Marketing Higher and Further Education

Marketing Higher and Further Education

An Educator's Guide to Promoting Courses,
Departments and Institutions

PAUL GIBBS & MICHAEL KNAPP

KOGAN
PAGE

First published in 2002

Kogan Page   Stylus Publishing Inc.
120 Pentonville Road   22883 Quicksilver Drive
London N1 9JN   Sterling VA 20166-2012
UK   USA

British Library Cataloguing in Publication Data

A CIP record for this book is available from the British Library.

ISBN 0 7494 3294 2

Typeset by Jean Cussons Typesetting, Diss, Norfolk
Printed and bound in Great Britain by Clays Ltd, St Ives plc

Dedication

To the ones I love.
– Paul Gibbs

To Dee for her
patience and forbearance.
– Michael Knapp

Contents

Contents

1

Introduction

[The UK brand of education] enables students to see the Britain of the 21st century; innovative, dynamic and the true leader in the new world order. British education is a first class ticket to life and I want to see that ticket given to as many people as possible. (Tony Blair, *South China Morning Post*, 27 January 2000)

We chose this quotation to highlight the central role that education and its promotion plays in a country's prestige and reputation. This comment by the British Prime Minister was not made in a political debate but at the launch of an overseas marketing campaign for British education. Educational marketing is of central concern and not just for institutional publicity departments. It is also big business. In the US, in the year 2000, the total expenditure per full-time higher education student ranged from about $32,000 for a full university course to $7,255 for students attending community colleges for two-year associate degrees. In the UK the figures reflect the lack of real diversity and limited private as opposed to public funding, and come to about £5,000 for most general courses, regardless of the type of institution.

A recent UNESCO survey indicated that institutions and governments spent about 6 per cent of their overall budgets on educational marketing, so a significant amount of money needs careful and targeted use. The fact that education is also increasingly a global business with rapid growth in distance learning facilitated by the Internet, the Web and e-mail will mean greater pressure to obtain value for money from marketing expenditure in the future.

The word 'marketing' often evokes feelings of concern, even mistrust, within the world of education. It is associated with sales, advertising and public relations. Educational practitioners, whose mission is vocational and who believe sometimes in knowledge for knowledge's sake, often feel uncomfortable and want to distance themselves from it. Marketing, however, is a *process* that can make a positive contribution to both social and economic capital. It is not just about turnover or profit; the experience and skills that we talk about can be applied where decisions on resources and on communications need to be made and implemented.

We think that it is essential to put the educational offering into the context of a marketing process, for it is the logical progression within the process that can help institutions understand who are their 'customers', how their needs are changing, and how an institution needs to adapt, develop and change to meet these needs. Without a systematic analysis of the context within which learning and knowledge is being offered and examined, scarce moneys spent on marketing can be wasted. The *Guardian* of 1 May 2001 quotes a report by the Council for Aid to Education that says voluntary donations of \$23.2 billion were given to US colleges and universities from the business sector, religious and other groups and alumni. In the UK it is thought that hundreds of millions of pounds are raised in this way, but there is no official record.

The same *Guardian* report revealed that the traditional 'old order' of perceived quality among universities has changed significantly. New names like the University of the West of England, Northumbria, Loughborough are appearing among the top 10 universities in the Quality Assurance Agency's list of universities with the smallest number of individual departments below the inspection threshold. The Open University shares eleventh place with the London School of Economics. There is even a University College (Canterbury Christ Church) in the top 20. So everyone is capable of playing on a broader stage and competing not just in the national markets but in world markets.

The pace and scale of change in recent years in the acquisition and use of knowledge means that the marketing practices of *focus*, *segmentation* and *customer satisfaction* have growing importance as the physical locations of institutions matter less and less. In order to survive, institutions need to understand what they are good at, what they can contribute, and how they can convince others that they provide quality, flexibility and content in order to add value and to become partners in sharing and shaping the futures of their students, researchers and benefactors.

In order to apply the marketing process we have to use marketing terminology, but we hope we use marketing terms in a way that is readily understood by a wide audience – not just marketing professionals. It is important for as many people as possible within an institution to understand how to use the marketing process to achieve their goals. This means everyone from Vice-Chancellor to junior lecturers.

We start by considering marketing as a strategic tool and then develop the specific implementation tools needed to achieve objectives successfully. This approach commences with an audit to decide who you are, where you are, and how you fit in (or do not fit in). The audit is a fundamental device that can also be used periodically as a monitoring tool to decide whether you are still going in the right direction or whether changes in the environment and 'the market' suggest a change or modification to the route.

One of the key audit skills is market and consumer research and that is the subject of Chapter 3. Having decided our destination or goal, we turn to how we should position ourselves in the market through the mechanisms of *segmentation* and *programme design*.

We follow this by considering the pricing of educational programmes and their promotion through advertising, direct mail and exhibitions. The field of public relations has a broad remit covering the reputation and image of an institution – not just its programmes – so it deserves a chapter all to itself. Advertising and promotion lead us on to the all-important issue of student recruitment and retention. Finance and funding are ever-present concerns, so we devote a chapter to the variety of ways that fund-raising can assist the development and progress of an institution towards its goals.

'Information and communications technology' (ICT), the Web and the Internet generally are having such a fundamental effect on the delivery and acquisition of learning and knowledge that we have concluded the book with a chapter on e-education and the changes it will bring to the ways in which we must meet the needs of the students of the future.

WHY MARKET?

Education has very complex programmes and products. Defining the role of an institution is not just a simple matter of identifying and attributing value-producing activity. The activities of higher and further education often involve highly intangible matter. The institutions themselves are motivated by real goals that arise from service and social responsibility, although the need to recognize the economic imperative is increasingly making inroads into this. An institution 'competes' in a market with other institutions but, unlike in other markets, it may have lacked or felt no need for the profit motive as a measure of success. Governmental and market pressures are changing this, and education's resistance to the professional marketer and the marketing process will fade as the sector recognizes its value in helping to shape its future practices. Diversity and focus will be the driving forces for the educational institution in the future, as its specific role in society is challenged by corporate global needs.

This move towards expression of diversity is recognized in the English Higher Education Funding Council's (HEFCE) 2000 policy statement on diversity, in which it speaks of mechanisms being in place for sustaining and encouraging diversity. These depend on 'the willingness of the Universities and Colleges to take opportunities to develop their own distinctiveness, and to use the discretions which current arrangements provide'. Diversity is a marketing notion and the HEFCE sees a diversified sector as one 'with the capacity to meet the varying needs and aspirations of those it serves: students, employers, purchasers of HE services and the wider community'.

There are four key areas that suggest that the appreciation and use of the marketing process can help significantly in shaping the future of the provision of education:

- *The complexity of the offering.* The product or programme encompasses an educational experience for the student, who is simultaneously a consumer of that experience. The product is also a resource provided to society for the development of other students. All other experiences, including support services within the institution, are value additions that enhance the student's ability to absorb and acquire the courses of instruction.

- *The complicated social role of educational institutions.* The independence of departments or faculties sometimes makes it difficult to add value through changes in practice and often requires significant resource investment, particularly when it involves distance learning, part-time participation and 'outreach' into community programmes.

- *The increasing importance of financial performance.* The institution must shape its market offering in such a way that it attracts investment – tuition fees, council grants, funding donors and others.

- *An approach to the market that sees students as informed consumers.* Students are not the homogeneous post-school cohort of the past. The increasingly different student segments – part-time, mature, distance learner, full-time, day release, online – need different market orientations. So the essence of the marketing process is to understand these differing consumer needs and adapt to them.

In answer to the question 'why market?' we would respond that we live in a consumer environment where the fulfilment of desires, whether they are valuable or not, structures our consumption habits as informed consumers. As educators we need to get our message through the clutter of competitive consumerism. Quite simply, we need to market our contributions. Marketing is a social and managerial process through which institutions and individuals obtain what they want through creating, offering and exchanging products and services with others. The management of that process involves the planning and execution of the concept and its related manifestations such as pricing, promotion and the distribution of ideas, goods and services in such a way as to create exchanges that satisfy individual and institutional objectives. In its broadest sense, it has to influence the level, timing and composition of demand in ways that help the institution achieve its strategic objectives. In order to do this it must bring together under a marketing plan:

● an explanation of the current marketing situation so that an institution can anticipate where they might be at the end of a planned period;

● a specification of the expected results;

● an identification of the resources needed to carry on the planned activity;

● a description of the actions that are to take place so that implementation responsibilities can be assigned, and monitoring set in place to evaluate the success of any actions taken.

During the course of the book we look in turn at the five steps in the marketing management process proposed by Philip Kotler (1999) in his very readable book, *Kotler on Marketing*. They are research; segmentation, targeting and positioning; the mix of activity; implementation; control and iteration. This is close to a simple definition of a project management lifecycle from initiation through definition to execution and then post-implementation review. The marketing research and then positioning and activity give purpose and depth to the management of the project. The only thing we would add at this stage is the need to assess risk – what can go wrong and what would be the cost – before finally moving into the implementation stage.

Marketing is a social and managerial process but it is also, and must be, commercial. One way to help the whole process, and demystify it, is to be inclusive in its planning and implementation. Good project management teams are multidisciplinary. So are marketing project teams. Run workshops, ask for comment and input from stakeholders. Involve as many people as possible – it will pay dividends.

STRATEGIC MARKETING PARTNERSHIPS

The now-ageing adage of 'think global, act local' has been given new impetus in education due to widening participation, increasing demand for knowledge skills and the removal of the protective barriers of time and space. Developments in information and communications technology have accelerated global collaboration and offer a springboard for future growth. Demand is clearly not just being met through the traditional university with its roots in a traditional liberal education. Recognition of the value of higher education has attracted new and less traditional students to seek higher learning, and institutions have to respond or be very sure of their existing positioning. Students want flexibility in delivery – they require online, distance learning material and programmes that match their needs rather than the needs of the programme designers, short courses, just-in-time programmes and credit towards professional recognition.

New providers are emerging into the learning environment to meet this demand, particularly in the US. Institutions like the University of Phoenix and the Western Governors University are leading the way. So have publishers like Pearson, McGraw Hill and Simon & Schuster by widening their core markets and entering into alliances with education providers. Global corporations are also reaching into areas of teaching and knowledge traditionally held to be the preserve of higher education institutions. In the US there are over 4,000 corporate 'universities' with their own associations grounded in an educational climate. Many actively engage in work-based learning, supported by distance learning, to offer first and higher degrees to staff to develop their skills and employability while increasing immediate productivity. In the UK, Lloyds TSB, British Telecom and British Aerospace are good examples. For example, the Motorola University gives its mission, role and objectives as follows:

Motorola University Mission
The University's mission is to be a catalyst for change and continuous improvement in support of the corporation's business objectives. We will provide for our clients the best value in leading edge training and education solutions and systems to be their preferred partner in developing a Best in Class work force.

Motorola University Role

Motorola University began in 1981 as the Motorola Training and Education Centre. During the eighties, Motorola University's charter was to help the corporation build a quality culture. The eighties also saw the establishment of corporate-wide training plans and training investment policies. By the end of the decade, the University had expanded its operations both in the United States and around the world. Motorola University also began offering new and more comprehensive services, such as applications consulting.

Since 1990, Motorola University has diversified further, establishing academic partnerships with institutions around the world. During a globalization process, the University has also implemented cultural design and translation services. Currently, Motorola requires a minimum of 40 hours a year of job-relevant training and education for every associate.

Motorola University is the strategic learning organisation of the corporation, complementing the training that takes place in Motorola's business groups. Motorola University is organised into regions and colleges with design teams to serve its customer base efficiently. The University manages 7 learning facilities around the world and has 20 offices in 13 countries on 5 continents.

Motorola University is staffed with a work force of 400 professionals. A flexi-force of 700 writers, developers, translators, and instructors provide services on an as-needed basis.

Motorola University Objectives

The University's objectives are to provide training and education to all Motorola employees to prepare them to be Best in Class in the industry; to serve as a catalyst for change and continuous improvement to position the corporation for the future; and to provide added value to Motorola in the marketing and distribution of products throughout the world.

Of course, many use the term 'university' seeking only to raise the status of their own programmes and many act as agents or in partnership with colleges and universities. Indeed the use of the terms 'university' and 'college' are in themselves problematic because many of what were the defining features are now shared by other institutions. Competition for lifelong learning provision from the private sector will continue. People may start to question what sets a university as an educational establishment apart from a corporate learning environment. Universities and colleges will have to be more aggressive in the way they market themselves with this much broader and global competition. To survive they will need to adopt the language and the nature of the market.

An institution's strategic plan must therefore recognize these changes, focus on effectiveness and efficiency and be prepared to change to meet the new challenges. This leads to the notion of partnership marketing with competitors, suppliers and customers. The seemingly contradictory coalescence of self-interest and collaboration, trust and accountability, competitive advantage and partnership may seem to create irreconcilable tensions. For years the recognition of the value chain in marketing and Michael Porter's notion of competitive advantage have focused on understanding and then controlling relationships with suppliers and customers. It could be argued that the value-added chain seeks only fragmentary improvement in the lot of the customer – rather, its prime objective is to beat the opposition. The difference for the world of education is that it does not try to beat others to achieve financial recognition for shareholders but delivers services to learners through quality education. There is a difference, and one that marketing techniques can support.

The future may depend on partnership in many forms. The process of partnership means a repositioning of the cultures of the partners so that efficiencies can emerge. Indeed, those parties within the partnership must see benefits for their own as well as the partnership goals to make it work at all.

To build responsiveness into partnerships between educational institutions as well as with commercial enterprises requires the following simple but institutionally challenging steps. They are built on the value inherent in the partnership, shared values of worth and the perceived benefits to each of the parties focused on the needs of the learners and their communities:

- *Top level support*. Make sure it is a partnership and that it is not perceived and believed to be a takeover. Cultures and goals must be similar. The recognition of complementary strengths must be evident. The whole must be better than the sum of the parts.

- *Institutional structure*. Structures must be in place that value the contribution of all. In a partnership a new institution is constituted. Systems and structures must reflect this. Partnerships involve change that needs to be actively and capably managed.

- *Respecting expertise*. Partnerships mean managing individual excellence within a team. Teamwork is the potential power of the new institution and, as the learner market has changed, so must the core competencies.

Success in any newly constituted partnership depends on its marketing focus. Above all, the process and techniques that we outline in this book are essential to ensure that the recipients of the partnership understand clearly at the outset what to expect.

The *Times* leader (14 May 2001), under the heading 'Lower Education', commented that the university sector is in desperate need of attention. It points to the sometimes wild and inconsistent reforms of the last 20 years steered more by 'political targets and Treasury edicts than anything remotely connected with scholarship'.

Importantly, it points to the variable quality of UK institutions, poor student/lecturer ratios, abysmal pay levels and red tape. It goes on to say that 'all universities are not alike and they must not pretend to be so. Less than 20 establishments secure 90% of research resources (the so-called Ivy League), but if government persists in a crude division between "teaching" and "research", establishments will never get decent lecturers for the former category … What is required is more concentration on students, and a light touch on universities from Whitehall.'

This is the strongest possible argument for the increased use of the marketing process for universities and colleges to establish unique and desirable positions in this incredibly important market, so that not just students but staff and funds start to beat a path to their doors.

The marketing audit

This chapter offers a number of practical instruments with which to audit your market performance. They are straightforward and owe much of their development to the work of Nigel Piercy, whose book *Market-led Strategic Change* (1992) is probably the best we have read in this area.

Marketing audits give snapshots of your relationship with your markets, both internally and externally, but they are snapshots of ever-evolving markets. Audits need to be carried out regularly to ensure that what you have done has had the desired effect and that unforeseen consequences and changes in your market can be reflected in your next initiatives.

Various audit forms are suggested below ranging from a simple 'do-it-your-self' audit of your various stakeholders to the tried-and-tested Ansoff and Boston matrix models. Other instruments suggested below help in dealing with the overall strategy as well as in the assessment of learner and corporate services. The final tool pulls together your overall objectives and tests whether your thinking is sufficiently well developed to give you confidence in what you are about to undertake.

JUST HOW GOOD ARE WE?

Many texts like our own will start with market strategy and lead into the hard slog of the market audit to ensure that you know where you are. Resource audits are not just one-off, up-front activities that belong only to the marketing team. Audits help to tell you where you are in the changing nature of your relationship with your market and its constituent parts. They also act as a way of checking expertise and information. They are a way to investigate the realism and purposefulness of your marketing and management information systems.

A REALITY CHECK

The first test is a simple one-sheet assessment of strategic objectives, comparing them with the reality of what you have achieved or want to achieve. It is best used with a range of partners in the marketing of the institution as it will show not only the gaps between strategic objectives and their implementation but also which of the public or stakeholder groups' perceptions of what is being achieved are most positive and which are not. This type of evaluation form is as valuable for corporate marketing strategies as it is for individual programmes. It is necessary to tailor the form for the specific marketing issue being investigated.

Form A (Figure 2.1) is a reality check, designed to look at the overall strategy. It can only carry snapshots of the views of those asked to participate. By separating the major functions, clarity of interest is made explicit. This analysis is not as detailed as the full audit developed at the end of the chapter but can give a good and quick overview of the success, not of the strategy, but of the implementation of the strategy. When using something like this, faults in the original strategy can become evident and this is a non-aggressive way of acquiring that information.

This form does not require expert knowledge; rather it assumes that the stakeholders' views are those of informed participants. This applies to the majority of the other forms presented in this chapter. When in doubt about a response go back and seek the additional information you need.

LEARNER SERVICE ASSESSMENT

Form B (Figure 2.2) is concerned with your learner service. It could also be applied to donor or corporate services. The form has a number of columns in order to allow more than one stakeholder group to state a view. The process requires the creation of criteria for successful implementation of the particular issue under review. The form is then given to particular stakeholders who rank how the institution performs on what they have previously considered to be the critical attributes for success in this area. Once this is

Strategy	
Completed by:	Time period:

Operational marketing policies	Strategic intent	Strategic reality	Strategic gap
Product, programmes and services			
Prices and value			
Communications ● selling ● advertising ● promotion			
Distribution ● channels ● logistics ● service			
Strategic positioning ● product/market life-cycle ● strategic position ● competitive positioning and differentiation ● customer satisfaction			

Conclusions/implications/actions

Figure 2.1 *Form A: a reality check*

Market/segment/learner group:
Time period covered: launch, annual review, others …

How good are we at each of these:	Marks out of 10 (1 = poor, 10 = excellent)				
1. Do all staff understand our strategy on customer service and quality?					
2. Do we have a clear and actionable service and quality strategy bench-marked against our competitors?					
3. Can we measure customer satisfaction and how useful it is?					
4. Do we have learner and satisfaction measurements linked to changes in our marketing policies?					
5. Can we and do we set standards for specific learner and corporate clients?					
6. Can we differentiate service quality or at least prioritise expectations?					
7. Do heads of department or course leaders set a good example in providing service and quality to customers?					
8. Do we have a way of working to remove obstacles and barriers to quality and service delivery?					
Total (out of 80)					

Figure 2.2 *Form B: assessment of learner and corporate service*

done your chosen stakeholders are given the list again and are asked to rank the importance of the service attributes. This weighting is applied to the ideal attributes and to the rankings given by the stakeholders on your actual performance. You have then obtained useful information that has immediate practical implications. You have the views of a range of stakeholder groups on the importance of your service and a crude weighting system so that you can evaluate not only where your offerings are low in terms of particular attributes but also what significance the group attaches to them.

CONSUMER/LEARNER MATRIX

The third of the evaluation forms (Form C – Figure 2.3) is similar in concept to the other two and focuses on your learner/customer relationship. The intention here is to understand your market segmentation.

Form D (Figure 2.4) is the customer matrix, a simple, cost-effective way of identifying any issues that the institution may have with its customers. What programmes do you offer (sell) to which groups? This self-analysis helps to identify where certain target groups are under-represented in programmes that were designed for them. It is a good reality check on the costs associated with developing programmes and the marketing that goes with them. It does not, however, just look at the figures – it attempts to reveal trends and clusters of programmes (target groups that have real resources so as to guide future development and budgeting). It can be very revealing, and when used with the Ansoff and Boston models (discussed below) it enables you to obtain a good picture of the institution's true position.

ANSOFF GROWTH MATRIX

This is still one of the best formats for mapping strengths and weaknesses. The Ansoff matrix (Form E – Figure 2.5) helps you to determine where your business is in respect of the development of its markets. The institutions given in this example have some very real opportunities and equally difficult choices. They may well have been able to maintain their different market positions in years gone by but today others may take stronger competitive positions and invade their markets.

It can be expensive to conduct this type of research formally but we have

Subject or market – ie chemistry or continuing education?						

Customer (eg part-time, adult returner, new student etc)	Programme clusters – full-time, part-time, short courses, bespoke, products, consultancy					
	1	2	3	4	5	Total
1.						
2.						
3.						
4.						
5.						
6.						
7.						
Total						

Figure 2.3 *Form C: product customer/learner matrix*

found that the Ansoff matrix can work really well by using a group of members from distinct stakeholder groups. By comparing the institution's competitive position with others on an axis of attractiveness of the programmes being offered, a map of the local/regional/national or global markets can be developed.

This is how it can be done. Simply consider the institution's competitive

Market:						
Customers/Products	1	2	3	4	5	6
1.						
2.						
3.						
4.						
5.						
6.						
Total						

This is a simple-to-use tool. Just list your customer and programme offers and ask a number of different stakeholders to score your success at satisfying them. Once the key stakeholders have independently scored on each customer progamme segment, use the chart as a stimulus to debate where you fall below acceptable levels and where you exceed expectations. Valuable lessons can be learnt from this reflective exercise.

Figure 2.4   *Form D: product/customer matrix*

position as high, medium, low or non-existent for each of the five following competitive attributes and allocate a scale to each of them:

● size of institutional enrolments;

● quality of students;

● quality of faculty;

Market attractiveness	Institutional strengths		
	Many	Several	Few
High			
Medium			
Low			

The Ansoff matrix in action

		High	Medium	Low	None
	High	A		B	
Market attractiveness	Medium		C		
	Low	D			

Business strength

Figure 2.5   *Form E: the Ansoff matrix, mapping your strength with the market's potential*

● reputation;

● growth rate.

By aggregating the scales for the programmes in the market (competitors' as well as yours) and then plotting them on the matrix, opportunities and threats to your portfolio appear. You plot them against the attractiveness of being in the particular markets. Assume that market attractiveness is characterized as low, medium or high and this ranking is derived from the following attributes:

- closeness to institution's mission;
- programme profitability;
- research rating.

The position of the institution on the matrix suggests the market approach it should take. It also reveals areas of weakness and strength within the institution and reveals its competitors or potential partners.

For instance, Institution A is in a strong position and must protect this from smaller institutions cherry-picking its best programmes. Institution B has attractive programmes but no distinctive positioning. If it cannot grow organically then it needs to shift toward the stronger position of A by developing new products, perhaps through merger. College C could be content, but should it want to improve its competitive position it needs to mobilize and direct its resources or it might lose its way or be taken over and lose its enrolments. The same threat exists for D. It needs to build up its stock of academic credibility quickly. At the moment its reputation is alive, but this will not continue for much longer given the more invasive performance management requirements put on institutions around the world.

Strategic decisions are based on where the institution wants to go. It needs to be clear on this and that clarity should work down throughout its structure. Successful management of this will ensure a focused institutional strategy that reveals clear marketing goals. We will discuss these issues further in the following pages.

THE BOSTON CONSULTING MATRIX

The familiarity of the Boston Consulting Growth Matrix (Form F – Figure 2.6) should not diminish its usefulness in the development of strategies to build on strengths and eliminate weaknesses (SWOT analysis, an analysis of the institution's strengths, weaknesses, opportunities and threats, and PEST analysis, analysis of the political, economic, social and technological drivers of these markets, should already have been done). The matrix helps to highlight points of strength and weakness but without the will to confront the often very difficult issues of an institution's historic positioning, which may now be regarded as questionable, the work put into the analysis can be painful. However, marketing problems need to be faced regardless of the short term pain – hiding from them can lead to institutions having to be responsive rather than proactive when they eventually face up to them. Audit and evaluation have led to great successes by marketers with flair. Figure 2.7 shows, in practice, what can be achieved by asking the hard questions and having the courage to respond effectively.

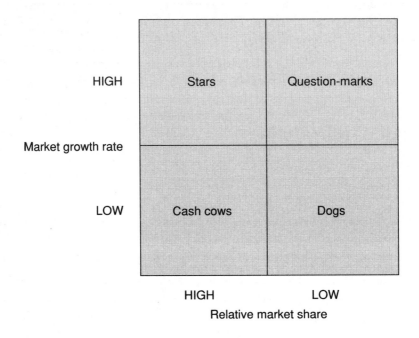

Figure 2.6   *Form F: Boston Consulting Growth/Share Matrix*

GETTING WHERE YOU WANT TO BE

The instruments offered are not as complex as a textbook marketing audit. They are not as time consuming, expensive or risky. As the programme outlined in Form G (Figure 2.8; another example is given in Figure 2.9) shows, a comprehensive audit has to scan across all the marketing networks of

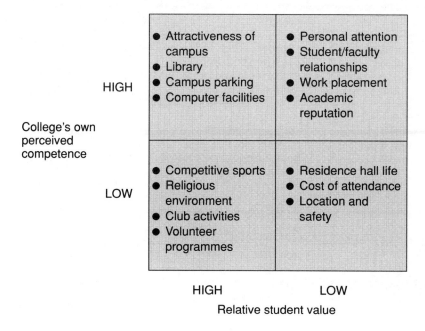

Figure 2.7 *Perceived competence and customer value*

the institutions and requires the use of considerable resources to ensure that good, useful information is guaranteed. The audit should not take on a life of its own. The purpose of the audit is to provide information for decision making and judgements, not to replace those judgements with data. We are not advocating 'flying by the seat of your pants' marketing – only that the resources should be spent where they give greatest value. So, when deciding on a comprehensive marketing audit, understand why you are doing it and what actions you are prepared to take once you have the information gathered.

Focus	Analyse	Objective
Learner needs and buying factors	Learner priority needs to be met through endowment and purchase. Customer group differences	Emphasize customer need not programmes, and the difference between potential segments
Programmes, learners and customers	Group programmes by their common need satisfaction characteristics	Create programme and customer definitions reflecting the marketplace: not access to own technology or internal operations
Key products and programmes	Identify the key products or programmes for each customer group/market	Establish customer group/market difference in product priorities
Marketing priorities and critical success factors	Evaluation of most important marketing mix elements for each group/market and the things the 'winners' get right	Establish relative effectiveness of marketing mix variables and competitive requirements
Market segmentation	Product/programme groups and customer types matching	Define customer- or learner-related market segments reflecting differences in customer needs
Institutional priorities	Compare each match of product and learner customer group to: • potential competitiveness • advantages this could achieve • attractiveness of this client group to us	Isolate areas of high and low priority and nice gaps and opportunities in segments, and then match to goals and capabilities
Market sizing and shares	Use emerging segments to value market and its trends, and share taken by competitors	Place values on segments to move towards targets

Figure 2.8 *Form G: the market audit (1)*

Focus	Analyse	Objective
Life-cycle and competitive position	Life-cycle stage and competitive position in each segment of programmes and products	Prioritize market segments and niches
Competitors	Evaluate: ● direct and indirect competition ● entries and leavers ● major competitors' characteristics	Identify competitive advantages and shortfalls
Marketing environment	Evaluate likely impact of broad changes in markets, law, institutions, technology, politics	Put planning into broader context of strategic change in the outside world
Market summary	Across the segments analyse life cycle stage, value, current business direction, priority products, marketing mix requirements	Choose priority market targets
Critical success factors	What must be right to achieve customer/ learner priorities to enrich the position wished for in mission	Specific action list
Marketing objectives	Develop in priority segments, the key marketing objectives and how they relate to sales and market share	Isolate major marketing goals, compared to corporate objectives and ensure they can be made operational

Figure 2.9 *The market audit (2)*

Market and consumer research

MARKET RESEARCH

Market research and consumer research help to define risk. They are undertaken to inform a decision to commit time and money to marketing goals.

Research can help to reveal some of the probable emotional and practical results of certain institutional behaviours. In general it attempts to provide objective facts that lead rational decision makers to a conclusion. However, it cannot make predictions with certainty and the decision maker's own judgements are critical to the consequences of the research. There is an important difference between preparing market research and responding to the results.

Know the risk profile of the decision makers and then design the research methodology to help them reach a conclusion. Plan ahead: too much or too little information, or too little time spent on analysis, can lead to decisions that are not relevant to the research brief, interesting though they may be.

Understanding the dynamics of your market is critical for long-term planning. Identifying the drivers of your particular market is not difficult. They are similar due to the structure of the society being investigated. The real skill comes in predicting the impact that these drivers will have on the marketing problem you are addressing. Capturing well-researched data, and identifying trends in them, form part of the management of information that is the spine of planned marketing action. The trend analysis that emerges from the investigation of the institution's macro-environment is then used alongside the results of monitoring the institution's internal environment in the form of enrolments, research funds and donations, to provide an enriched understanding of who your customers are, what they will want and how fit you are to provide it.

Kotler (1999) suggested that there are five trends that underpin markets and, by understanding trends revealed by research, valuable contextual information for marketing decisions can be gained. These trends are:

- demographic;
- economic;
- lifestyle;
- technological;
- political and regulatory.

Demographic trends

The most helpful thing about demographic trends is their predictability. By understanding the average age profile of the student population on the different programmes that you offer, for example, the size of the potential market can be plotted and tracked as it changes. Major trends such as changes in the numbers of physically active yet economically inactive mature citizens can suggest opportunities such as the provision of fully funded short courses in subjects related to their leisure interests.

Economic trends

Trends in wealth creation and distribution will have direct effects on the provision of education and the form in which it is provided. As the education system becomes more of an explicit provider of skilled workers for skill shortages, good planning will be able to predict how to prepare for future demand. Economic trends change the demand for different types of educational programmes. In good economic times consumers want to know how to develop themselves and their spending power, whereas in poorer economic times they want to be able to reskill to obtain or retain employment.

Lifestyle trends

The trends captured under this heading relate to people's interests, activities and opinions. Education is a lifestyle product and one that we are being encouraged to use throughout our entire lives. The needs of lifelong learners change as their circumstances change and can be segmented in meaningful ways so that marketing communications can be devised to support learning experiences that are relevant to the needs of complex learners. The learner, of course, may fit into more than one segment at once. The example in Table 3.1 is a segmentation developed for an examination body offering awards across the main educational provision arenas.

Table 3.1 *A basic customer segmentation matrix of the learning market*

Learner Segments	Characteristic	Delivery
Natural gateway/ status learners (full-time)	● Know education is a means to an end ● No natural breaks ● Successful ● Demanding of results	● Educational institutions ● Support through the Web
Gateway learners (part-time)	● Value educational for progression in employment/status ● Focused purpose – goal orientated	● FE/community college ● Distance learning ● HE ● Work place
Just-in time learners	● Immediate need/reward ● Employment orientated (craft, skills, information) ● Recognition important	● FE/community college ● Employers ● Teaching providers ● Distance – online
Leisure learners	● Learning for its own sake ● Qualification is secondary – recognition important ● Retention poor	● Educational and other institutions ● Clubs ● Web
Disengaged learners	● Learning is a turn-off ● Not intrinsically important	● Bite-sized learning ● Flexible/Open ● Readily available
Non re-engaged learners	● Lack of motivation to progress or broaden education ● Lack of confidence not ability ● No perceived need	● FE/community college ● Outreach ● HEI outreach ● Community group
Basic skills	● Education has failed them – therefore afraid of re-engaging ● Strong life skills	● FE/community college ● Community schools

Technological trends

We are all too aware how these trends affect all aspects of our life, lifting barriers of time and space in our interaction with others and with things. In the educational context, technology allows students greater control of their education processes. This can put enormous pressure on academics who communicate online and through e-mail. Technology leads to more demanding students who not only want to study when they wish but also want to engage with experts when they want. Delays of a day in answering e-mails become almost unacceptable!

Political and regulatory trends

In the UK, the government has placed education at the centre of its political credo. This brings resources but also greater explicit accountability as government ministers strive to show that their particular spin on education is reaping results in particular ways. In the case of the UK, they are attempting to create increased economic prosperity through an increasingly skilled population. This emphasis on education has brought with it an increase in regulation, political initiatives and funding, which need to be complemented by cohesion, direction and strategy. Perhaps the new learning and skills councils will do some of that, but this will only occur if there is joined-up thinking in the strategy-setting regional development agencies and central government.

CONSUMER RESEARCH

Consumer research is a multi-million pound enterprise with an established role in business decision-making. It has, over time, been proven to add real value to marketing decisions when it is used appropriately. Consumer research can be put to use in many arenas: to measure market potential; to determine market characteristics; to aid long-term decision making and forecasting, and to contribute to other marketing functions such as product development and advertising. In our context, research can assist decisions in many areas, for example:

- the development of new programmes or qualifications;
- understanding existing student attitudes;
- providing insight into the perceived reputation of institutions with their stakeholders – employers, schools, parents, students;

- planning the style of a new prospectus or department flyer;

- judging the appeal of the institution to alumni or to other potential contributors to the institution;

- engaging the support of employers or other interest groups, directly and indirectly, perhaps informing your public relations strategy.

To start to understand your customers, look for common characteristics. Finding this information and then using it to attract the type of student you want (or that the government asks you to recruit) can be a time-consuming task. One way around this that has effective results for further and higher educational institutions is to profile students by using the information that is locked away in their postal addresses. The practice of profiling your student cohort, linking this with the programmes you offer and then offering the same types of programme to a similar profile of future students sounds compelling. This process can increase programme suitability in a cost-effective way. Some of the key findings of a 1999 study by the Further Education Development Agency (now the Learning and Skills Development Agency) were:

- that it is possible to analyse characteristics of a college's student population against its catchment areas with comparative ease;

- that these procedures can be applied to specific categories of student – for example students can be categorized according to mode of study, ethnicity and specific courses;

- this reveals significant differences between colleges as well as within them;

- information obtained can be used to improve perceptions of a college's ethos: it can help tackle operational issues such as marketing, staffing and community relations.

The emphasis on decision makers is important as it keeps the focus on action related to research. It is this focus on the need to understand why the research is being done and what the outcome that the research results will influence will be that helps shape the questions asked.

The decision to use research, whether it is a large or small research project, needs clarity. What are the uses to which the outcomes are to be put? What is the level of risk the research is being used to manage? What is the cost and can the confidence conferred by the research be obtained from other, cheaper sources?

Figure 3.1 offers a schematic view of the research process. It tries to ensure that focus is kept not only on the research process but on the value that it will add to the marketing decision that it is intended to inform. Throughout, it helps to keep these four questions in mind:

- What is it that you want to find out?
- From whom?
- Why?
- At what cost?

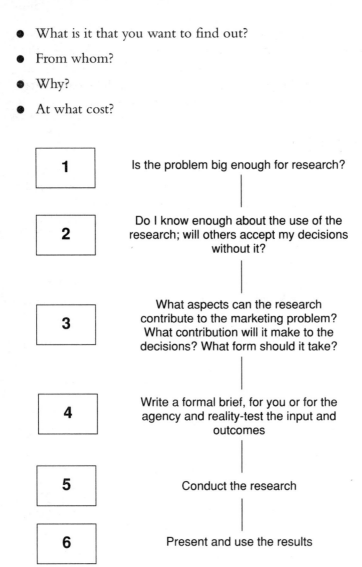

1	Is the problem big enough for research?
2	Do I know enough about the use of the research; will others accept my decisions without it?
3	What aspects can the research contribute to the marketing problem? What contribution will it make to the decisions? What form should it take?
4	Write a formal brief, for you or for the agency and reality-test the input and outcomes
5	Conduct the research
6	Present and use the results

Figure 3.1 *The research process*

Should I research?

As a precursor to the resolution of any problem, particularly a marketing problem, a rational individual will consider if there is sufficient information upon which to act. We do not carry out research every time we make repeat purchases, for example, but when the decision will have a great impact, or has emotional involvement (a house, a car, a new political affiliation), we need to make extra effort and we research in more detail. We research at two levels: the impact of the purchase (does it satisfy us) and who is best able to satisfy the goal. The outcome and modelling of purchasing behaviour will be considered later but for our purposes it is difficult to recognize the difference.

How to approach the project

The nature of the research can vary from discovering the preferred colour for the Vice Chancellor's ceremonial gown to a full-scale national opinion poll research report. The decision is based on existing knowledge, evidence of success and the distance (in terms of change) the actions that are being researched go beyond what is known and accepted.

The issues are really quite simple: should we repeat last year's media schedule, did it achieve what we wanted, shall we change it? What has changed: customers' use of media, the costs, the level of recruitment needed, the external environment or attitudes of those controlling the resources?

Given that research can add value either to the market process or to gaining the decision to go ahead, the next stages are to:

- define the research objectives;

- redefine objectives in terms of the budget available;

- write a brief – do this regardless of who will carry out the work (yourself, colleagues or outside agencies) and remember to state the form in which the research results should be presented;

- ensure that the timetable is reasonable and effective (timely and well-developed research is helpful; late or rushed research is not);

- use the research as many times as you can to ensure maximum value for money. (Obvious? Well no – many companies have huge numbers of research reports that are never revisited for new projects because they are not labelled as being specific to that purpose.)

The contribution research can make, and writing the brief

Regardless of who is doing the research, clear guidelines are required before undertaking the activity. This is obviously more important when a third party is undertaking the research, for you have less opportunity to change the process when it is happening. Even if you are doing the research yourself the brief is an excellent reference document.

Good research briefs will include the items outlined in Table 3.2.

Table 3.2 *An outline of a typical research brief*

Objectives	What is the purpose?
	Inform others in their decision making, stand on its own for public relations, inform an advertising campaign or prospectus design.
Scope and methodology	What can really be achieved?
	Research often does not solve problems but it reduces the risk in the decision.
	Ensure that the research is able to do the job asked of it – it cannot replace personal judgement.
	Make sure the research is fit for purpose.
Costs and logistics	Keep to your budget and redefine the research to fit it.
	If the value of the research falls to a level with the cost, either don't do it (for it is clearly not important enough) or find another method to achieve your objectives.
	Define time scales for delivery of draft question-naires and discussion guides.
	Arrange for interim briefing.
	Define the format of the final report.

RESEARCH METHODS AVAILABLE

Most marketing textbooks discuss the basic division into quantitative or qualitative research and in, practical terms, these are usually interpreted as requiring questionnaires or focus groups. We will say a little more about these later, but first we should make it clear that the research method used should be that which is most appropriate for the task of collecting the data you want. Do not use focus groups when you want a statistically valid response on launching a new programme. Do not use a questionnaire to secure an understanding of what is meant by enjoying distance learning.

Qualitative research

The essence of qualitative research is to be diagnostic. It seeks to discover; it probes rather than counts and it mainly uses in-depth interviews and focus groups. The most important thing to remember here is that those looking for a percentage response will find it hard to believe the conclusion you reach if it is based only on this form of investigation. There is not much you can do about it other than just accept it and redesign the methodology. The techniques involved in this form of research are not those used in general discussion-group management. They are skills to be learnt, and they require practice. This is extremely important because the method demands more than surface responses from respondents. The objective is to go deeper and find motivations and values that would not be readily articulated in conversation. This form of research uses projective instruments to understand the meaning held by respondents. The best people to administer and interpret these instruments are those who understand the process – trained market researchers. These techniques are used to overcome barriers to responses, which include awareness, irrationality, self-incrimination and politeness. A summary of qualitative research techniques is given in Table 3.3.

Quantitative research

The more neutral methods of collecting data that are less sensitive to interpretation is based on questionnaires and the accurate recording of the findings in a form that is statistically valid. This has a real advantage in offering a measure of respondents' past behaviour, which superficially influences future decisions. But remember that these methods are not suited for exploring complex new ideas because time and cost factors do not usually allow for building an understanding of the issues being discussed.

There are many skills that need to be mastered to undertake this form of research. Asking an inexperienced researcher to write a questionnaire for telephone research can prove very expensive when the results reveal that the responses you collected have little relevance to the problem that you thought

Table 3.3 *Summary of qualititative research techniques*

Format	Projection techniques to elicit modes of perceiving the world:
	● sentence completion
	● word association
	● cartoon completion
	● collage
	● repertory grids
	● role play
Administration	● In-depth interview
	● Focus groups
Main purpose	● Reveal meaning, language and motivations. Elucidation of respondent's reactions where these are not easily expressed.

you were investigating. Table 3.4 summarizes some of the issues of which you should be aware.

Mail is possibly the cheapest way of getting to respondents but it is not necessarily the cheapest way of eliciting responses. We prefer telephone, Web or direct distribution in lectures with collection at the end of the session (high return but not too good for sensitive issues).

Presenting the findings

Research only has real value when it is used to inform the marketing problem that it was set to illuminate. To ensure that it adds maximum value it needs to be presented in a way that supports the decision you have reached. A pre-meeting with the researcher to determine which parts of the research are particularly important, who will be responsible for the presentation of the results, and the format of that presentation might well facilitate this. It is important that the research should be enlivened by a context and by its relationship to the problem that it is addressing. This task is for the research commissioner. Without a considered approach, the expenditure on the research can be wasted.

Table 3.4   *Summary of quantitative research techniques*

Format	• Closed- and open-ended plus attitudinal questions – the former are easier to analyse but not so rich in information.
	• If you use open-ended questions, ensure you have a workable coding system.
	• Sampling – understand the size of the population of your target market and design, if necessary, appropriate sample stratification, size and sampling error.
	• Ensure questions are understandable to the audience (not you), suitable for data retrieval and that respondents will be willing to complete them.
	• Avoid bias – in content, wording, order and sequence.
Administration	• Mail – drafting is very important, use for larger groups, need to understand non-response, respondent self-administered.
	• Telephone – speedy, flexible but expensive although may be cheapest per respondent.
	• Personal interviews – expensive and best for free response, open-ended questions, dependent on interviews.
	• For in-depth analysis the number of interviews ought to be around 400 and for snapshot analysis about half that.
Main purpose	• Descriptive

By clearly defining the research objective and planning the use of the research, important risk-reduction benefits can emerge for your marketing plan. Research cannot answer your problem – that is a matter of practical judgement – but it can improve the decision.

USING THE INTERNET FOR RESEARCH

The Internet can be used in a number of ways: conventional discussion groups, online groups, and e-mail groups.

Conventional groups

These are ideal for the early stages of idea generation. You can use your own site as a stimulus for discussion. You can present information in a number of formats to engage with respondents. The numbers included can be extensive. There are problems, of course, not only in terms of people dropping out but also in terms of access to the Web and in leading the group. There is also little interaction. However, it can be cheap and responses can be easily managed.

Online focus groups

There is more interaction with respondents who react to instructions online. Indeed, other colleagues can follow the way in which respondents react to instructions and stimuli online.

Usually these groups are conducted in a chat room. The best group size is small – about six. The main technological problems revolve around ensuring that everyone has visited both the stimulus site and chat room. It also helps to have a technician at hand, particularly if the group will have to follow an uncommon procedure.

Table 3.5 gives a few of the advantages and disadvantages of this approach.

Table 3.5   *Comparison of the benefits and problems with online focus group data*

Benefits	Problems
Able to reach difficult groups	Non-verbal inputs
Cheap interaction projects	Lack group dynamics
Real time group	Less client involvement
Perfect transcript available	Security
Clients can watch	Attention

E-mail

This approach has been well developed in the US where traditional listserv and Web-based bulletin boards are common.

Traditional listserv

This enables a private mailing list to be set up so that members of the group can easily send messages to each other. Moderation is often difficult particularly in conversation that can be dominated by a few people.

Web-based bulletin boards

This approach centres on a Web page with a bulletin board. The moderator sets up a subject for discussion and people post replies. Daily e-mails can be sent to prompt responses and these can be confidential.

Advantages of the Internet

- Speed – the Internet is much faster than either phone or post. It really is worth trying with appropriate sample groups.
- Cost – it has been estimated that it could be up to five times cheaper than postal questionnaires.
- Efficiency of data collection.
- Options of online reporting as it happens.
- Using the Web for interviews can be very effective.
- It is easy to fill in well-designed interfaces.
- You can include graphics and use sophisticated functions.

Finally, when considering e-mail or Web for surveys, Table 3.6 might aid decisions.

Table 3.6 *Comparison of the benefits of using e-mail and the Web for research*

Consider e-mail for:	Consider Web for:
very short interviews	very long surveys
better response rate	complex counting
staff and student response	visual audio input
recruiting for Web interview	Web related

4

Market segmentation, 'taking a position' and seeking differentiation

SEGMENTATION

Customers – students, academics and other stakeholders – have different needs and only some of these can be satisfied by any one institution. Customization is increasingly breaking down markets into groups with smaller, more specific needs. (However, while this fragmentation of the mass market may well be true in Europe and the US, in other parts of the world – including Russia, China and India – education still has a mass market to aim for with all the substantial benefits this can create.)

Segmented markets have three main characteristics:

- enhanced value, which can lead to higher profit;

- a better match with customer needs;

- the ability to exclude those segments that do not match the student/ programme values.

They can be identified or created through:

- benefit segmentation – for example, the availability of low prices or short courses, job relatedness, relevance to recreational interests, immediate recognition for use in the market;

- demographic segmentation – for example, socio-economic grouping, ethnic origin (this is most often favoured by government for it reinforces their notion of centrally controlled social justice);

- lifestyle segmentation – for example, continuing professional development for students or lifelong learners.

Many segments can be revealed by observing the attributes of certain student groups. Institutions can target one segment or many segments to develop the most appropriate proposition.

In the UK, for instance, the notion that learners, particularly mature learners and those from the lower socioeconomic groups, see education as a means to an end and not just an end in itself, has an enormous effect on the type and form of programmes that institutions have to offer. More than that, it makes students behave as traditional customers for a service. They want extra value and today most of that value is in the external worth of the accredited award(s). In this, education has explicit external value calculated as rates of return over the working lifetime of the student. Education is up-front money and tuition fees.

Once segments have been identified, the appropriate form of communication can be developed for the targeted audience. Promoting a short evening programme on stock market options for retired people would require a different approach from that which would be used to attract child care assistants to enrol on a diploma in child care. This segmentation approach does of course mean that the 'brand' of the institution has to stretch across both propositions so as to enhance them in this competitive environment. Moreover, the decision to run both programmes must not devalue the brand and reduce its reputation.

When segments show that they are viable by displaying the characteristics of stability, accessibility and profitability, then these segments can be managed. Success in segment management is determined by the increase in market share in the particular segment and the income that is associated with this growth.

To be successful in segmentation marketing it is essential to know the segments, to understand their needs and to target your services and promotion in ways that motivate, add value and increase your reputation over time. This builds confidence that your institution can deliver.

POSITIONING

Positioning the institution in a market place that is becoming more crowded with educational offerings from a wider and more diverse group of suppliers involves fulfilling customer needs in the best way possible in a particular market. A market can help shape the efficiency of an offering, whether it is a health product, education, or basic human rights, provided customers are aware of the range of offerings.

We must not assume that the goal of the player is necessarily to gain advantage over others. To illustrate the difference, we might consider two market-based philosophies. The first and perhaps best known is that derived from the analysis of Michael Porter – competitive advantage. The second is customer advantage.

Competitive advantage

By seeking competitive advantage in patents and technical expertise, and by creating uncertainty, and exploiting a lack of expertise in suppliers, the market leader can determine the nature of the market and flourish. It can even do this to the extent of combating the power of customers to seek products and services on terms they want rather than on the terms that the suppliers to the market want.

Customer advantage

The second way of engaging in a market is to seek excellence in the offering to the customer and to allow customers to determine who should flourish. By exceeding customer expectations equity is built into the reputation the market for education has both in general and in particular institutions. The consequence of this is that institutions' customer bases increase as the value added to the experience by dealing with the institution increases. In this approach core competencies, partnerships and relationships dominate and the instruments of strategy – analysis, implementation and monitoring differ as they relate to specific segments of customer needs.

The difference between competitive advantage and customer advantage is summarized in Table 4.1.

Table 4.1 *Summary of the difference between competitive and customer advantage*

Competitive advantage	Customer advantage
Secure market against competition	Secure a relationship with the customer that secures your market position
Strategies to pursue competitive advantage	Strategies to enrich customer value added
Analysis of market in terms of power points and try to reduce other market participant powers and enrich your own	Analyse market position in terms of your strengths and weaknesses from the customers' perspective
Market forces	SWOT (Strengths, Weaknesses, Opportunities, Threats) analysis

THE EFFECT OF COMPETITIVE STRATEGY ON INSTITUTIONS

We need to consider the quest for competitiveness and the impact it makes on the institutions. Institutions have basically three competitive strategies, two of which involve using resources better – by market domination or cost advantage – and a third that looks to do things differently.

An institution whose discourse is competitive advantage to gain market dominance has two routes to achieve this: it can do so through differentiation or through cost effectiveness. It can restructure its portfolio, or reduce its headcount, making it smaller, less costly and more focused. It might redefine its market.

The second approach is based on the premise that, as a smaller, more focused organization, you can be better in a particular area than your competitors – in research, teaching, or in outreach into the community. This approach requires the re-engineering of processes and continuous development of the way in which the organization deals with its environment. Such strategies attempt to improve the organization itself. It clearly has major short-term advantages for staff and could enable the organization to dominate a sector or, at the very least, have sufficient market share to benefit from economies of scale.

The third approach is the really challenging one. It involves embarking on a process of reinvestment and regeneration strategies in an attempt not to live in the past. The outcome of this is an organization that is different. An example of this is Regents College in the US, which is making use of technological leadership and online assessment to offer a global service to certain selected customer segments throughout the world. Neither of these approaches need apply to the whole institution. They could apply to a department, or a programme or a qualification.

Doing things differently

In order to change the way it does things both successfully and radically, the institution must give up a preconceived notion of how it maintains itself and how it reacts to the external drivers in the market place. Institutions need to be flexible and able to respond swiftly to the demands of their markets. This might well mean the removal of the notion of academic boards if they are associated with long lead times. It might mean abandoning the notion of appropriate working hours. It could entail different ideas of student-guided learning time or, indeed, perhaps new ideas of what pedagogy actually is.

The four development phases of a market occur most of the time, and knowledge of the location of the market helps institutions to place their offerings to the customers appropriately. Following convention, the four phases are:

- emerging;
- high growth;
- mature;
- declining.

We can use these tools to analyse the market at a number of levels. If, for instance, we take the notion of adult literacy or higher education as a sector then the former is in the emerging market stage and higher education is the high growth phase, at least as far as the UK is concerned.

This framework has equal validity at the institutional, school or department level. Table 4.2, for instance, contextualizes the four phases in a department or school of business.

Table 4.2 *The market development phases characterized for educational organizations*

Phase	Characteristics
The emerging market	● A new market triggered by an innovation that offers a perceived, superior benefit. Initial sales grow mainly in learners keen to be seen as leaders. ● Wireless e-commerce
High growth	● New learner segments, more offers of products and market share might be more relevant. ● E-commerce and IT
Mature market	● Not many new entrants; price and service become important as capacity to sustain all suppliers becomes evident – basic IT training without Microsoft certification
Decline	● Volumes are set for permanent decline: need to exist or develop resurgent growth through new products and users. Renaming or repositioning traditional qualifications.

The four stages are generally sequential but can alter depending upon the product and the gap between each phase. Before planning the strategies in each of the phases, it is most important to understand where your service or product lies in relation to the dynamics of its market. For instance, a product that adds no discernible value when compared to established products in a market with high geographical coverage is unlikely to succeed if the market for the service or product has reached a mature or declining position. However, if the market is still to be fully satisfied or defined then the new entrance of a university offering with a sound reputation can not only find a useful and profitable niche, but its mere presence can add substance to the market and make it more attractive to a selection of new learners who would previously not have been attracted to it.

One of the most effective and well- known ways of looking at an organization's portfolio and its markets is the Boston matrix. This can be helpful for visualizing the state of the programme or services that the institution is offering. Figure 4.1 shows a Boston matrix with some example programmes and markets.

Once the portfolio is understood, the next thing to do is to understand the 'drivers' of the marketing process you are engaged in. So how do we discover the drivers?

Internal drivers

The marketing transaction matches your needs with those of learners. You need to understand what they want. This is covered in our discussion on market research. The other dynamic is what you want. How many learners do you need on the programme now and into the future (developing the market, cream tomorrow – depending on your perspective) or what image do you want to create with your existing and potential learner base? How will you

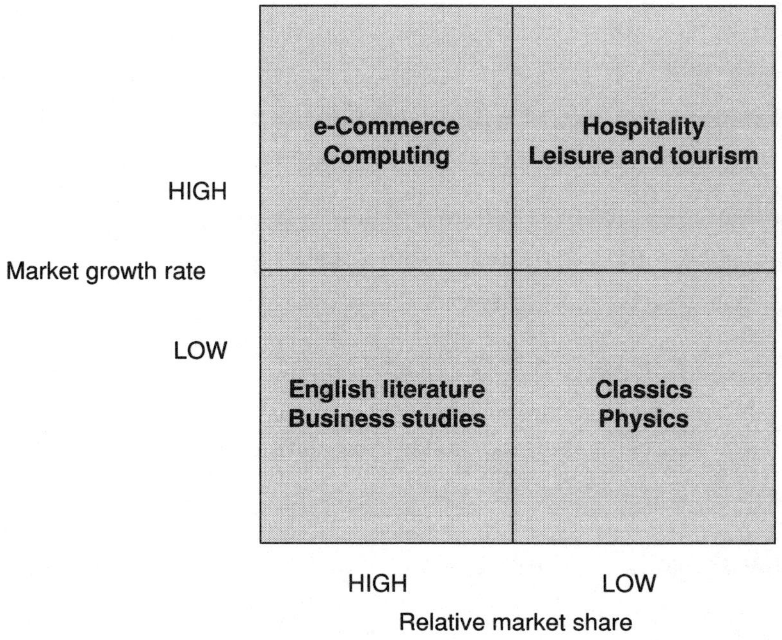

	HIGH		LOW
HIGH Market growth rate **LOW**	e-Commerce Computing		Hospitality Leisure and tourism
	English literature Business studies		Classics Physics

Relative market share

Figure 4.1 *Boston matrix*

45

know when you achieve it? How much of the budget can be set against it? Is the programme more to do with indicating a new direction/image of the department than immediate recruitment? Does your job depend on the outcome?

Resolving the internal drivers is not too difficult if you can be honest in reflecting on the issues. It is an important aspect of all marketing exercises. You need to know not only what you are doing but why. This might entail moral decisions (just let this learner on the programme and take the money even though I know it will be beyond him in two months) and financial ones (whether to drop the price marginally or reinvest any surplus in colleagues' pay or equipment). The balance between the ethical and the financial is a difficult issue. The motivation is clear – yours and yours alone but the internal motivation will contribute to your energy and success. If you are not committed to the service or programme you are marketing, a significant gap appears in effort and efficiency. You should know your needs and be honest about the purpose of the marketing exercise.

External drivers

An understanding of external drivers can be within your control or outside it. So the first thing to do is to establish what is what, track what you cannot influence and get on with what you can do. This can mean hard decisions and you might need to take a good look at how the competencies of the institution are aligned with its marketing environment.

There are many models of PEST (political, economic, social and technological) analysis and most are just checklists of issues that ought to be considered in understanding the current and future drivers of the market place into which you are offering your product or service. Such an analysis is worthwhile in any marketing exercise but its level and intensity should be appropriate to the purpose of the exercise.

Market analysis

One way to examine external drivers is through market analysis:

● Consider the variables that could affect your market? Usually they will be political, legal (regulatory), technological, and cultural.

● List these – do this in a team and cover as many current and future issues that you can – don't forget the positive ones!

- Once you have collected them select the top three in each of the key areas.

- Map them on a matrix with 'effect on your institution' along one axis and probability along the other (see Figure 4.2).

- If you want to go further, you can ascribe a percentage probability to events and therefore rank their importance to the institution.

The result is a chart that tells you what to watch, where to expect disappointment and where to ensure you have anticipated the effect of the event.

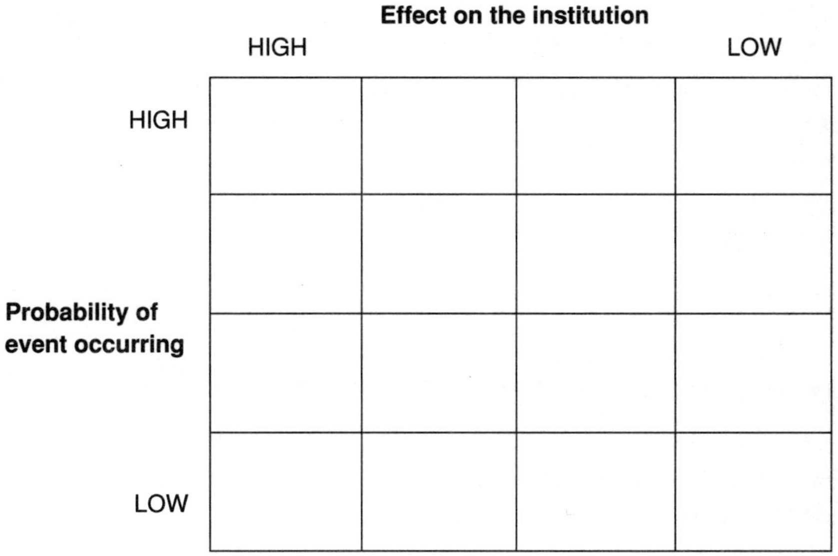

Effect on the institution

Figure 4.2 *Risk assessment matrix*

DIFFERENTIATION

At the level of a particular academic course or programme, differentiation might be very simple – a demand is recognized and no one else is meeting the demand in a particular way. This demand might be for a new course in investment trusts, the latest Microsoft software or garden design made easy. Examples of differentiation at the programme level accumulate and affect the overall positioning of the institution.

In marketing, differentiation can be achieved through product, image, personality and service. There are three interlocking notions to be considered when evaluating your existing position and deciding on how to hold that position or move to a more sustainable and differentiated position:

- the position of the institution/unit;
- the themes that this generates;
- the differentiation process.

These three issue combine to offer us a ranging of positioning options that are then checked against the institution's mission, vision and objectives. The core capabilities of the organization, its history or legacy, its current values and the perceived characteristics of the institution and its portfolio of brands influence the informed response that the institution makes to these options.

These considerations combine to create the institution's image, or images. It is important to understand the variety of images that the institution's audiences have of it. Any institution has a number of images, including the image that the institution's leader wants its users to have and the actual perceived image. It is important to know whether there is a gap here and then what to do about it. A simple test involves constructing a list of what the institution and its individual departments think their position is regarding the status of their education provision, or the responsiveness of its administration to learner and employer needs. Ask representatives from four groups – staff, students, governors and employers – how they rank the institution (and department) and what other criteria they would use to describe the institution.

If there are any serious gaps on a 10-point scale (anything in the region of two points is potentially problematic) investigate and plan to close the gap.

Differentiation can be achieved in a number of ways. These can be clustered into four main categories: products, image, attitude and service.

Products

Products, whether we use the term to cover services, short- or long-term education or training courses or programmes, all have a core function. It is the job of the product developer to build distinctiveness in to the products that are offered to customers. If they were left undifferentiated no value would be added to them by different institutions. This is indeed a threat in education where over-prescriptive regulators, inspection regimes and government intervention restrict innovation and creativity in curriculum design.

The quest for differentiation should not blind you to the importance of the consumer's analysis of how well the product is delivered – its performance at the functional level. Programmes also need to stand the test of time. This is particularly true in education where rates of learner and employer adaptability are slow. What new and existing programmes must supply is desirability, fitness for purpose and validity, for education is a lifelong activity.

But given that a market does exist, institutions have to blend characteristics that supplement the programme's basic function. These features ought not serve solely to satisfy the teacher's or lecturer's own sense of fun or innovation. To add value, they must be evaluated against the perceived worth to learners and the cost of delivery.

Image

The second differentiating aspect is the image of the institution, of the product, and of the outcome. This is both the tangible image of symbols used in written and visual communication and the intangible notion of the institution's atmosphere, its presence. The combination of tangible and intangible symbols to present a successful image is critical and a skilled aesthetic job.

Modern logos might be conceived to attract new young participants into higher education, but is this what most want on their certificates? Or is a more traditional recognition of their success more important to them? Colleges need to know this. Other aspects of image relate to the relative positioning of the institution with others. Cambridge sits well with MIT or with Microsoft, but does the image of other universities benefit from post-modern designs on tee shirts in the style of, say, beer advertisements?

Attitude and service

The third and fourth aspects are more concerned with attitude and service. Academic and other staff often select institutions using criteria other than their desire to contribute to the institution's ability to develop and maintain successful transactions and relationships with the institution's target customers. They must show that they share the culture of the institution and project the image of the institution. This manifests itself in the service that they provide to match learner expectation in terms of delivery and maintenance of the programmes. Quite simply delivery needs to be timely and appropriate. Those who have been involved in Internet tutorials know how demanding this can be.

Keeping programmes fresh is a new problem given the ease with which information can be gained from the Web and the speed with which technology changes the processes that are being discussed. Extra teaching and online tutorial time sit uncomfortably with keeping up to date and pushing forward the barriers of knowledge. Something has to go, and, with the global market place bringing a much wider range of solutions to learners, the marketing challenges are larger than ever before.

BRINGING IT ALL TOGETHER

Names

Marketing researchers have suggested that a good name should be short and memorable, should say something about the key benefits, should be easy to pronounce and culturally neutral.

Symbols

Logos and symbols encapsulate the brand's image and make it stand out. Many new universities have decided their logos partly by drawing from the traditions associated with awarding degrees and partly by considering the need to appeal to a younger and wider audience. Certainly as programmes become more vocational the crest and shield is being replaced by stylized, minimalist designer symbols.

Narratives

How does the institution tell its story? Does it have a vice-chancellor, principal or a chief executive? Is academic dress worn for dinner? Are the corridors used as galleries for student works or those from the institution's own collection? Are the dining areas integrated for all staff and learners or are there differentiations that send out messages of worth?

Concepts

The notion of Oxford University or Harvard University creates a concept of élite education that is appealing to certain student and employer groups. New universities create an altogether different concept and the change of name from 'polytechnic' has failed to alter it. Concepts of 'new', 'vital' and 'innovative' can come from the buildings, as well as the delivery of programmes. The Open University enshrines a concept of accessibility that evokes a certain idea of its students as part-time, hard-working people who attend summer schools.

Discussing branding, Trevor Thorne, Director of Marketing and Public Affairs at the University of Surrey, suggests that the main problem facing the development of higher education brands is lack of proper commitment to market research. He comments that few universities employ market analysis (even further education colleges) as part of their marketing process. He adds that there is a lack of commitment by staff to the brand of their university. In response, universities need greater focus on their branding activities by understanding better what is being brought from them in terms of their customers' aspirations, and they need to deliver what is needed, not what the institution wants to deliver.

5

Programme design

USING CORE COMPETENCIES

Designing new programmes can be the most exciting part of the marketing of education. It can also be the most ineffective use of resources if the issues of cost and practicality are an afterthought. Programmes need to make money or at the very least have some other benefit for the institution. They must contribute to the overall positioning of the institution.

The tools used in the development and monitoring of programmes will produce information that needs to be assessed in the context of the missions of the institution. For instance, local learning partnerships that are intended to fill skill shortages have a defined target. Once fulfilled and future demand is estimated, resources might be less profitably employed in this arena of activity than in another. Knowing this and being able to shift the resources easily to another area of opportunity will be central to the institution's long-term success. In this context the cultural value of programmes is not as important as the institution's ability to serve its most lucrative markets. It is no use arguing that a programme has merit for civilization and humanity if what is desired and funded is technologically driven skill. Institutions have a choice between independently funded or state-directed programmes. They can also choose the form in which they are delivered, up to a point. However, the new UK credo of 'education, education, education' is followed very quickly by education for economic success with explicit accountability. These changes are not so dramatic in the college sector, which has a tradition of invasive inspection, but will take some getting used to in the universities.

DEVELOPMENT: SUSTAINABLE OR PROFITABLE?

The most basic decision that any institution has to make is what programmes and services it will offer its learners, alumni, donors and other interested parties. What it offers establishes the institution's identity, positions the institution in the mind of its customers and determines how they will respond to the offering. Most institutions, therefore, have a programme/customer segment mix (even if they have not actually articulated it as such) and a number of product lines (clusters of products designed to suit certain needs). These products may be analysed in terms of their core, tangible and augmented offerings. The first two of these create the product brand and the addition of the third changes the brand from a product value proposition into a distinct organization/customer value proposition.

Core offering

As the term implies, this is the essence of the offering and can be different for different customers. For instance, is the core offering of higher education higher learning or employment? The recent vocational foundation degrees seem to be positioning employability as the core offering and they have marked similarities to the US associate degrees but do not centralize the liberal study aspects so much. Simply stating that the foundation degrees will lead to employment is not enough, however; the processes to make this happen need to be fixed before the programme is launched. The two critical issues for core benefits, then, are that they should have clarity and ensure that the product delivers.

Tangible offerings

The tangibility of education is primarily concerned with the wrapping it is given. Basically the tangible offer has three characteristics that are blended into the product brand: feature, quality and packaging.

Features might include free access to the Internet, discounted material, individual tutorials, photocopied lecture notes or notes on individualized CD-ROMs. Features have the advantage of being easily added or dropped and need to be kept fresh because once they become commonplace they cease to add value to the product offering.

Quality is the domain of inspectorates and other agencies – the guardians of the shape and value of the outcomes of the education process and hence the quality of the teaching. There are, of course, opportunities to exceed expectations – to develop the experience of learning so that students take up its existential qualities of choice and opportunity. This requires teachers to go beyond the current popular competencies model and to seek to help students participate fully in their own change process. Indeed, this is something that distance learning offerings, that are unsupported by face-to-face engagement, fail on. (This is one of the reasons why the Open University, with its supported seminars, tutorials and summer schools, is so popular and successful.)

Finally, you need to consider the packaging of the programme. Apart from the explicit communication that the institution has with its stakeholders, the state of its physical location can contribute greatly. Clean rooms, carpeting, regular washroom cleaning, all set a context in which the individual learner comes to understand who he or she is in the context of the learning experience.

Branding

The notion of a brand has been central to strategic marketing for many years. Doyle's (1994: 159) definition declares that: 'The specific characteristic of a successful brand is that, in addition to having a product that meets the functional requirements of consumers, it also has added values that meet certain of their psychological needs.' A brand should confer symbolic meaning and value upon its user (see Mick, 1986; Flaherty, 1987; Belk, 1988). Confusion can occur when individuals from one social system encounter a brand that has symbolic meaning for another. Here the brand carries the expectations of the host group and the aspirations of the excluded group, and can act as a barrier to inclusion in a desired lifestyle. In this, the brand's image has value when it sends a message about the involved that is desirable and worthy of the consumer's investment. The aspirational point of higher education, grounded in its liberal values but reconstituted as a gatekeeper of employability, may have significantly changed the values of the brand and the reaction of certain stakeholder groups to the symbolic as well as economic benefits conferred by a university degree.

Little has been published on the marketing of a system to its host community although the British Council (1999) completed a project on the image of higher education overseas. This interestingly focused on its perceived conservatism and not on its lack of quality. The basic texts remain Ryans and Shanklin (1986) and Kotler and Fox (1995) (there has of course been significant literature on the marketing of individual initiatives, of which these are a selection). Although much has been written about organizational trust, less has been written about the notion of a brand and its trust relationship with its customers (see, for example, summaries by Gurviez, 1997; Hess, 1995 and O'Malley and Tynan, 1997).

The view that brands are conceived inside organizations but that their success is decided by consumer perceptions is presented in a model by De Chernatory and Riley (1997). Although the model has much to say about the internal management of the brand response relationship within the mindset of the consumer, it is driven, in their opinion, by the confidence of the consumer: 'The more favourably consumers perceive the brand, the more likely it is for a trusting relationship to grow, further reinforcing positive attitudes. The overall effect of this should enhance the value of the brand to all stakeholders' (De Chernatory and Riley, 1998: 1,086).

So why hasn't it already happened? Research shows that the notion of marketing is associated with the attraction of students to the university but that the ability to write deliverable marketing plans below the department and dean level within the university sector is poor. (The *Journal of Educational Management and Administration* has run a series of articles on the practice of marketing as an educational management skill. See for example James and Phillips, 1995.) The problem is deeper than mere ineptitude: there is a lack of trust in marketing. Johnson (1996) produced results that show the disengagement of UK academics from the process of marketing. She concluded:

> Some academics will accept the market and with it marketing, albeit perhaps in a rather limited way. Others in varying degrees may see marketing as incompatible with their ideological perspective. Others may accept the pragmatic. Few if any see it as an activity to which they should give any more than nominal attention. None saw it in the wider 'relationship marketing' terms. (1996: 73).

One approach is to change the narrative from the managerial model of Kotler to the marketing mix framework discourse offered by Bruner (1988), which, based upon the softer version of the 'four Cs' (these being; concept, cost, channel and communication – see Wasmer, Williams and Stevenson, 1997, for an application in higher education) may hold more sway with intransigent academics.

When building a product brand, then, the following considerations should be borne in mind:

● remember that you are not the target market;

- market research gives you recommendation clout;

- money is helpful, but personal contacts, tenacity and perseverance are equally important;

- it is helpful if alumni can be involved;

- you will not please everyone.

When we move to the augmented brand, what we are doing is bringing all the product brands under the rubric of a customer value statement that is made manifest through the alignment of the institution's processes. This may sound obvious but things may have to change as customers demand change. For instance, the desire for shorter programmes that are part-time, accessible and delivered at times that are convenient to learners, recognizing their prior achievement and a range of other requirements that service providers in the non-educational world have had to accommodate, may change the culture of the institution. Clearly some institutions will be able to hold the line a little but if state funding follows the student, and if commerce calls more of the shots in the form and content of the curriculum, those institutions that do not re-engineer their processes to add value to their customers will really miss out. (See Maklan and Knox, 1998, for an interesting approach to marketing.)

THE PROGRAMME DESIGN PROCESS

What is really important in the programme design process is the culture for innovation. In the post-modernity of the twenty-first century, fragmentation and discontinuity are the contexts in which educational programmes emerge. This means that even five-year validation periods might be too long. Regulatory pressures as well as the needs of employers are hard to predict but will be far more important for funding and for satisfying customer demand. Innovation and creativity are attributes that we want to engender in our learners, so it is logical that we exhibit them ourselves. Innovation is not, then, a once-a-term or once-a-semester thing; it is constantly forming a background against which we undertake our professional activities. In such an environment the real task is to capture ideas, evaluate those that are good and that match the competencies of the institution to exploit, and then get on with them!

As with most processes, a chart can help to identify the stages that can enhance the chances of the new concept/service/product being successful (see Figure 5.1).

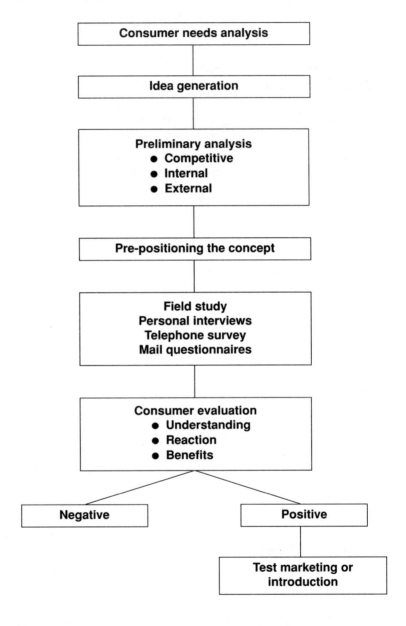

Figure 5.1 *Systematic new product development*

Consumer needs analysis

What do your existing and potential markets want that you are in a position to deliver with added value? This links with much of what we said about positioning and market research. The trick is to blend the knowledge, insights and feelings that we have with the identified needs of the market. Clearly your customer base has certain requirements of an institution like yours. You need to find out what these are. Real benefits can be obtained where we find a new area of programme content, delivery or any combination of the many things that motivate learners to engage with you to learn. This might mean that what you see as the strength of your position is not theirs. Why are you teaching in a particular college or university? Do you think those reasons are the same as those of your target market wanting to study at your institution?

Idea generation

There are many ways to generate ideas. They can be basically divided into ideas that come from within the institution and those that come from outside it. In the first category will fall ideas brought to the institution from overseas visits or foreign exchanges (faculty and students), partners and suppliers to the institution. Internal ideas can be generated through suggestion schemes, student surveys, think-tanks, complaints, environmental changes, brainstorming, post-project evaluations and student projects. Wolverhampton University's engineering degree programme came from such an idea and the associate degree work of Birmingham colleges was generated from links with the Chicago Washington Community College.

If you want to be more sophisticated you can use techniques such as programme checklists where attributes are listed and then rearranged to see if they can suggest the need for other products or whether existing products can be applied to other subject areas or consumer groups. Other analyses include value chain, morphological and gap analysis. For a good basic text on idea generation see Sowrey (1987).

Preliminary analysis

Not all ideas are good. For you to decide to take them further they need to pass through a number of gates. These ensure that the programmes add value to the institution's brand, enhance the relationship with the target group, can be delivered profitably or, if not, then that they at least form part of the institution's strategic plan. This analysis is internal and external, looking at the needs of the institution and of the potential customers. Without clear reference to, and guidance from, the institution's mission, drift can occur and can ultimately make the institution something that its core processes are not aligned to deliver. This is also an opportunity to test your products against competitors' offerings. You may well feel that you need to match the competition or be distinctive from it with a particular offering. One important gate here is that of the ethical position of the institution. Regardless of the market potential, if the proposal could lead to those running or participating in the programme using the experience for activities with which the institution would not want to be associated, then this is a chance to prevent it. The ethics of marketing, as Laczniak and Murphy (1993) discuss, ought to be and are becoming recognized as important by consumers. When dealing with young people we need to be extremely alert, for instance, to issues of political or social manipulation.

Pre-positioning the concept

'Well, we hardly ever get it right first time!' This phrase highlights the need to reconsider programmes and adjust them to what we know. Often this will not require any major surgery but the changes can be critical to the programmes' success. They can help us to tighten the target market and be certain that the resources allocated to the programme are used effectively and will be sufficient to ensure a successful experience for the learner and the institution. Those ideas that survive need to be developed into something that can be understood by the market place. Particular aspects of the programme are tested, for example the length of the period of study, the level of the programme, where it will be taught and how much work experience will be accredited. These are just some of the issues which might influence its attractiveness to the market. Stakeholders have an important role at the field study stage, where local employers, their representative groups, professional bodies, as well as those expecting to take the programmes, need to be consulted. All this information is considered within the institution's decision-making processes before a decision is made to commit resources for full development and promotion.

Field study

This can be omitted if the cost of failure is less than the cost of piloting. This might well be the case, for example, for a short course in 'managing your investments' that is being developed out of lectures given to students, and promoted with a one-colour flyer to local residents in detached homes. It would be a very different matter if the project were the development of online delivery of an MBA programme. Testing here would be critical because the development and promotion costs would be significant. To find that the programme's modules are wrongly targeted or poorly designed, thus failing to match the expectations of the learner, could be much more expensive.

Consumer evaluation and institutional response

Once the programme is launched then its success ought to be measured against the previously agreed launch criteria. This should then lead on to an explanation of what has happened. The evaluation is needed whether or not the launch has been successful. It is as important to know the reasons for your successes as it is to understand your failures in order to prevent repeated mistakes.

This does all take time, and opportunities can be lost. It is important to ensure that the reputation of the institution is not compromised, and that the process of product development itself is kept under review so as to ensure that the process is rigorous enough to reduce the risk of failure. This last point is important for in other sectors many more programmes fail than succeed. Research, as we have already shown, can help us make the correct decisions but it can work against us by delaying decisions and letting the prize go to another. This is as important in education as in any other market and the evidence shows that product life cycles are getting shorter and development time faster. Make sure that your product development process is fit for its purpose, enhancing and not handicapping your activities.

New products are not, as we have often said, stand–alone activities. Often they form part of a portfolio and they enter markets that are in a number of different phases of their development. These issues are discussed next.

ANALYSING THE EXISTING ACTIVITY PORTFOLIO

The mission of the institution should give a very good idea of what the port-folio should look like. If it does not, then it needs a thorough overhaul. The product and activity portfolio must match the wishes of the institution's markets. It must also reflect the business side of the institution. It should be possible to determine what the distinct goals and markets of the institutions are by inspection of the activity plans of its departments or faculties. If this is not the case then something needs to be done. The first task for any review of the product portfolio is to ask the question, 'does it reflect our distinct positioning?' 'Which programmes don't achieve this and why are they part of the portfolio?' The answer could well be that they may indirectly contribute to the status of the institution, which then allows the other programmes, closer to the mission of the institution, to increase their currency in other fields.

The second stage is to look at the contribution that the programmes make to the overall goals of the organization. This is then coupled with the third phase, the analysis of the relative position of programmes in the programme portfolio. Traditionally this is achieved by combining knowledge of probable trajectory of the programme's own life cycle with its current position. This analysis can be done by plotting enrolments, applications, career opportunities and by understanding competitor activities. For instance, by comparing the product cycles of classics and information technology programmes you might expect to see a decline over time in one and an upswing in another. Information technology programmes are clearly in a growth phase, philosophy at maturity and classics retreating into the safety of a few dedicated institutions.

Figure 5.2 illustrates the phases of the life cycle and maps the profit profile on it as well.

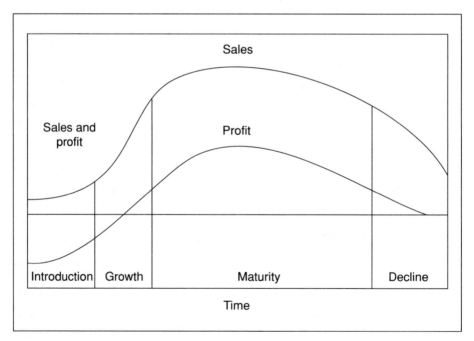

Figure 5.2 *Sales and profit life-cycles*

Within each of these product cycles the locus can be described in terms of four stages:

- introduction;
- growth;
- maturity;
- decline.

First stage – introduction

Figure 5.2 shows that the introduction, when the product or service is introduced to its market, is a period of slow growth. The slowness of the growth may depend on the degree to which the market is being expanded, new customers are attracted to existing products, or a new product is being introduced. It is the last group that usually takes the longest to take off. Customers who usually purchase in the introduction stage, where the product demand is unproven, could be termed 'early adopters'. They either have vision or see novelty as reinforcing their own self-images. Either way, purchasers in the introduction stage take a much larger risk than those who wait for the new product to become established in the market. This risk is shared with the provider, for neither can be sure that the latent demand identified by the research will materialize. The programme may yet to be proven as a route to employability, may fail in gaining acceptance from employers, may have elements yet to be fully resourced or may be in a medium that is not available to all. This last, of course, could have been applied to Web-based courses only a few years ago, but this delivery channel now seems to reaching most learners. The risk may be balanced by the price that can be asked or some of the cost might be borne by the government.

Second stage – growth

The second stage is further growth in the market take-up of the programme and this is where you would expect it to enjoy rapid market acceptance and begin to generate a substantial return on investment in development. This is due to increased numbers of learners taking the programme but adding only small variable cost to the fixed set-up costs that have already been spent.

Third stage – maturity

The third stage is where the programme enjoys an established position in a stable market but a slowdown in growth occurs because the product has found an acceptance in the purchasing habits of the learners. At this stage profits stabilize but are susceptible to the action of competitors to take market share. Indeed it is at this stage that market expenditure tends to concentrate on sustaining market share. Profits can be high but you need to recognize how long the programme can hold this position. If its content or the fashion for learning its represents is about to change it can absorb inappropriate levels of resource. This is because the normal direction from maturity is decline.

Fourth stage – decline

In decline, sales registrations fall and it becomes important to ensure that the full costs of running the programme are known otherwise the programme may run at a deficit before this is recognized.

Within each of these categories different programmes may be at different stages. For instance, continental philosophy may well be in a growth phase while programmes in early Greek are seen to be out of their 'useful' phase.

However this is not always sufficient. To analyse market maturity at the discipline level will give a broad indication of the most attractive sector but within each sector the individual programmes will also exhibit their own lifecycles. This might mean that a classics programme will need limited change every five years whereas an IT programme may need to be completely rewritten every three years. The lifecycle might be even shorter for skills-specific programmes where the rate of change is determined not by the institution but by commerce.

MARKETING INTERVENTIONS

Marketing interventions can have an impact at each of the stages of the lifecycle. Even in our previous example, Classics programmes can be revitalized by external influences – a new musical movement or an innovation. Old attributes of programmes can be linked to more contemporary issues. Shakespeare and Plato have opened new markets in the sales of business books and universities offer consultancy and other services in the commercial world.

Of course, the product lifecycle has its weaknesses. There is no common

shape so plotting positions into the future is not easy; there is real unpre-
dictability in the turning points and it is because of this that your professional
judgement is required. To remove a programme too early will cost money. To
support it too long will lose money. A more forward-looking approach is to
understand the institution's core competencies and compare them with the
attractiveness of future market opportunities. By building a matrix it is
possible to evaluate the institution's current portfolio and to identify areas
where it might be advantageous to develop. Indeed, on the same matrix you
can plot the portfolio content of competitors and see if they know something
about the market that you don't!

The portfolio of any college or university offering a wide range of
programmes and services can be mapped. Figure 5.3 gives an example of such
portfolio analysis. The size of the circle gives an idea of the relative size of the
income/students/research funds generated from this activity compared with
the rest of the portfolio.

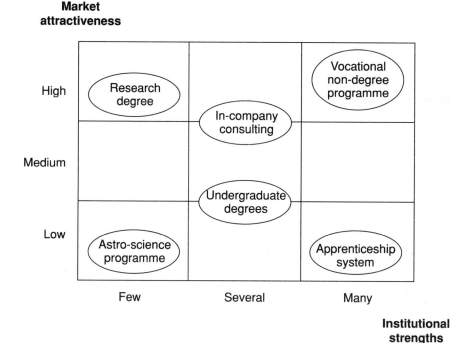

Figure 5.3 *Portfolio analysis provides map of present business*

The example in Figure 5.3 would indicate that any strategy that tried to develop a position for this institution based on research would quickly be in difficulty because its real strengths are in vocational education and training. For an institution bearing the title 'university' this might be hard to face if the management is living in a false world of Oxford spires.

6

Pricing educational programmes

Can a particular programme make a profit? Is it viable? Does it help the brand? As we approach a new funding mechanism through the new UK learning and skills councils and other funding councils, the ability to set appropriate fee levels becomes a more important part of the educational marketing mix.

Pricing involves much more than just stating a price for a programme based on the costs of delivery. To set a price accurately requires an understanding of a number of related issues, including the relationship between pricing decisions and institutional missions, how the learner and the purchaser view the price, and how the customer judges the value that it conveys. The price should maximize tuition revenue whilst retaining the institution's mission for inclusiveness.

Issues that affect pricing include 'bite-sized learning', costs of assessment, 'hop-on-hop-off' delivery and 'payment as you achieve'. There are also issues of who pays and how. Will individual learning accounts allocate higher education funds? Will the new learning and skills councils have wider influence and flexibility than the earlier separate college and work-based funding routes? What role will employers play in providing day-release and directly funding students (particularly on programmes that deliver value to the student but not immediate value to the employer)? And of course there is the Web and the importance of direct learning.

Price is an extremely important attribute of a programme. It differentiates between brands and between the value of the different offerings but also allows the institution to function according to its plans. Fixed prices for all programmes funded by the state or by corporate or personal investments will match the cost-recovery demands of some programmes but not others. In these circumstances colleges and institutions need to determine not only programme but portfolio pricing strategy so that the whole mission of the institution can be manifest in the programmes it offers its public. Pricing is not an isolated act; it is a constant monitoring of the relationship with consumers to understand where increased revenues can be claimed and where excessive prices are reducing income or changing the positioning of the institution. Once intuitions have a sound basis for the costing of their activities, they will be able to point, on the one hand, to funding gaps in research and teaching and on the other be better able to price the real cost of research and other services they provide. The move that many institutions have made to activity-based costing enables them to decide how much an activity costs before a decision is made to finance it. In the UK a small working group has been set up to assist in the provision of such information. It is called the 'Joint Costing and Pricing Steering Group' and its work has wide implications for marketers.

Competitor pricing can, and sometimes ought to, influence the pricing of an institution and its decisions also influence others.

THE PERCEPTION OF PRICE

So what does the price convey to purchasers? Above all else it is an indicator of value. This value may be intrinsic to the programme or it may be related to the benefit that studying at the institution conveys. It is in this difference that the investment made in the quality of the institution exceeds the commoditized value of the learner's outcomes and it is here that increased margins can be made. This is the argument made by the Russell Group of elite UK universities for higher tuition fees for entry to their universities so they can invest in better staff and resources to maintain their leadership position. They follow the Ivy League example set in the US, although the different nature of primary funding allows a higher level of bursary awards there. Such institutions evoke national pride in benchmarking themselves as a national resource that needs to be kept distinct and fit to compete with international rivals.

The margin between costs for the institution's tuition, corporate identity, research, time and resources and the cost of enrolment for the learner (savings, lost work opportunities, scholarships) is the net benefit or surplus gained from the transaction. The institution gains by being able to undertake its core function and so build its reputation, to employ existing scholars and to nurture others, whereas learners enhance their job prospects and enjoy prestige and personal development opportunities. Figure 6.1 illustrates the model of the equilibrium price where both parties' needs and requirements are balanced in the price. This 'fair' price is made up of all the real costs of delivery plus a margin that represents the added value or benefit of this particular transaction.

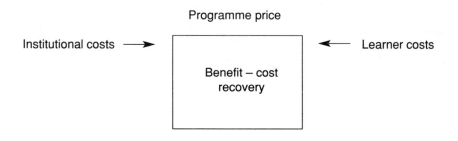

Figure 6.1 *A model of perceived value in the price*

BENEFIT RECOVERY

It is not easy to calculate the variable costs attached to a specific programme and even less easy to understand whether it is making an appropriate contribution to the institution's overheads. By using a variety of methods of management accounting the institution can understand its cost structure in different ways. Resolving this is an issue for the financial director or Pro-Vice Chancellor.

This leads us to the obvious conclusion that to set an appropriate price for a programme, the institution needs sufficient information to understand the costs it incurs in running the programme. This is often complex and will involve considering direct and indirect costs (both of which may be either variable or fixed) as well as the direct and indirect benefits that running the programme may create.

If the actual costs are known then the managers can reflect the value that the learner attributes to taking the programme at the institution. Accurate internal cost information is necessary to make informed pricing decisions. However, many financial reporting systems are not set up to reveal data easily in this form. Programme, faculty and student costs can be dug out of the accounting systems but this can take a great deal of time. Marketing-friendly accounting systems are needed. In order to achieve this you need to let your financial director know what information you want to obtain easily and on a regular basis. Remember that most accounting systems are put together to serve the needs of the finance department in producing monthly and annual accounts; you will need a different perspective in data presentation.

PRICING BY REFERENCE TO COMPETITION

Another way of positioning price is to assume that others have it right. Competitor pricing by matching, lowering or increasing your price sends a message out about the quality of your programme (which, once delivered, must match or exceed expectations). If the programme is unique then it can command more and if the institution is prestigious the same programmes can be charged at a higher price. Research shows that consumers often use the price of a product or a service as an indicator of its quality.

Indeed, learners tend to rely on price more frequently in making decisions if they lack confidence in making that decision. This is the essence of premium pricing for brands where the brand's reputation provides the confidence the consumer needs. In practice, learners will also compare prices that are significantly less than for comparative institutions and this may cast doubts about why they are so low. Learners are likely to conclude that this is for negative rather than positive value reasons, particularly if they are unfamiliar with the institution's reputation. Figure 6.2 makes the point in general terms.

| | | Price | | |
		High	Medium	Low
Product quality	High	Premium	High value	Superb value
	Medium	Overcharging	Medium value	Good value
	Low	Rip off	False economy	Economy

Figure 6.2 *Pricing messages*

PRICING TACTICS

The traditional approach of one price for all might be favoured by the government, but this doesn't have to apply to fully costed public or private programmes. A number of different pricing approaches can be adopted that might better reflect the change in structure of the education arena. In this we follow Kotler and Fox (1995) who suggest 11 different pricing tactics, of which we think eight are relevant here:

- *Unit pricing.* There is a set fee per module. This price will be for tuition, with assessment and certification costs added. It provides greater flexibility for the student, allowing payment as learning progresses. It does have problems in reducing the predictability of year-on-year income but it is surely the way the market is going.

- *Two-part pricing.* Here the student has an enrolment fee to the institution that covers the resources and facilities. Students then pay more on top of this for every programme they take. It should encourage students or companies to take more programmes as the cost of corporate resources of the institution are charged only once.

- *Term or semester pricing.* The student just pays for a time at the institution. No further fee is charged for any programmes taken: it is an all-inclusive fee. This can have a negative effect on quality as students may try to cram as much into as short a period as possible.

- *Differential pricing.* Differential pricing works when different segments of students can be identified that show different intensities of demand. For example, differential pricing could fail if different prices were set for programmes delivered during the day and lower prices set for the evening, if the day students decided to attend in the evenings. Differential pricing has important policy issues for the institution, which need to be resolved before using this approach.

- *Negotiated fees.* This to some extent is how UK higher education tuition fees are set but, instead of the student negotiating directly, his or her parental income determines the price to be paid. Of course, discussions with employers lead to real negotiations and to be an effective negotiator on behalf of the institution you need to know the real costs of delivery.

- *Quantity discount.* This is useful for part-time students being sponsored by their organizations and for in-house programmes that were originally priced on a *per capita* basis.

- *Time discounts.* This is 'pay early, get a discount'.

- *Peak-load pricing.* This approach is not used much in the UK. The demand for resource use determines the cost of the resource. The highest bidder gets the best slot.

The potential free market in educational fees in the UK is a question of great debate. It clearly has political as well as marketing implications.

7

Promotions – advertising, direct mail and exhibitions

The education market is well established as a global phenomenon. This is certainly true in the major English-speaking nations: Canada, the US, Australia and the UK. The adoption of the market with its implied managerialism at all levels of education has affected curriculum design and has created the need for educational institutions to use the techniques of the market. These include image management in what Symes (1998: 134) calls the 'symbolic economy'. Indeed much of the work on the symbolic economy has originated in Australia where the application of semiotics to the iconography of education institutions has revealed very interesting changes and insights into how they wish to shape their discourse with their publics.

Much of this discourse is set against the state's desire to rank everything. This ranking on the same scale of outcomes is designed to ensure that everyone can be held accountable against the same standards. As Blake et al. (1998: 2) have pointed out, 'this in turn entails the devaluing, and perhaps the eradication of what cannot be ranked'. In the UK, schools are ranked in gigantic league tables according to examination results, and university departments are ranked in terms of their research and teaching performance. Progress is demanded, but then criticized if it reveals lower standards. The power of the simplicity of managerial accountability over the complexity of the educational project certainly holds sway in the UK and we see very little difference elsewhere in the world. We live in an educational environment of anti-intellectualism and a suspicion of the motives of theorists, questioning their pragmatic competence and directing hostility towards their ideas. This is evident in the attitude of our student customers and in the ever more influential employers and their organizations.

STRAPLINES AND SLOGANS

In the struggle for student numbers and to secure a funding base that is more stable and less dependent on the state, universities and colleges have adopted more aggressive strategies in their marketing approach. This has led to an increase in advertising on the Web, in newspapers, on television and in cinemas. Most is slick and professional and the notion of brand development is evident as each institution seeks to differentiate its offering from those of others. And it needs to be. Increases in student fees increase the demands on the institutions from their student customers who want explicit returns for their investment of time, energy and money. This applies whatever the programme is. The state demands choice and the customer, directly or indirectly, is empowered to pay for it. This has led to slogans such as:

- 'A university for the real world.' (Queensland University of Technology)

- 'Why bother with a course that won't get you a job? We don't.' (North East Surrey College of Technology)

- 'A university of applied learning.' (Leeds Metropolitan University)

- 'After all, it's your choice.' (Cheltenham and Gloucester College of Higher Education)

- 'Preparation for life.' (De Montfort University)

- 'With the right education you can do anything.' (Napier University)

PROFESSIONAL APPROACH TO IMAGE AND COMMUNICATION

Colleges and universities have now set up infrastructures to provide the professional service required to manage impression marketing, and this is symptomatic of the move to switch from the cultural to the mercantile approach to education. Education is now positioned and aligned to general patterns of consumption. It is a commodity and is therefore subject to the same criteria of consumer satisfaction and evaluation as other purchases. To compete in this market, the prospectus and the Web site have taken a key role in the interface between the institution and its future students. In this the prospectus has moved, we believe, from the handbook of old to the advertisement of today. It has been refashioned to capture the concerns of the potential student. It is now more upbeat. Some prospectuses even tend to downplay the university as a place of study and intellectual challenge. We are not saying that all have changed, for the more established colleges and universities have retained their version of academia – Harvard, Oxford and Cambridge for instance. But many institutions, particularly the newer ones, have reached out for the endorsement of employers and past students to create an image of youthfulness, and this is reflected in their iconography. The practices that are emerging from institutions provide insights for a public well versed in the imagery of consumerism.

The image management of the sector reveals that instrumentalism has become a pervasive feature of the ethos and academic aspirations of many institutions. So how can we go about creating these images and what stands behind them to our publics?

COMMUNICATION AND THE USE OF ADVERTISING

Every organization is cast in the role of communicator and promoter. These simple insights of Kotler apply to the educational sector as much as to any other. Indeed more so if the values that most educators hold are to be adequately respected by their public. The traditional ways in which these messages are communicated are through the promotion mix, which has four key elements:

- advertising;
- face-to-face promotions;
- public relations; and
- personal selling.

When planning the strategic objectives of any communication activity a mix or blend is needed between all of the following:

- the strategic goals of the institution;

- competitive advantage through competing for visibility;
- positioning of attacking existing markets or market entry;
- the desired customer response.

Decisions need to be made about who the audience is, what relationship is intended with them and how best to get to them. For instance, if the audience is pupils at schools then the communications strategy might be more effectively targeted at the school's careers officer directly. An alternative approach might be to heighten the awareness of the institution with employees to such an extent that they carry your message to the training manager in their company. Either of these strategies can be effective provided they are well planned, well implemented and are part of a well co-ordinated overall plan. Getting to the target market is critical for successful marketing and this plus the size of the potential market will determine the media used.

We do not intend to spend too much time discussing the development of great advertisements and the use of particular media because most institutions have a professional marketing department and this will want to control the usually large proportions of the marketing budget spent on this activity. They are the ones to consult if you require advertising or any promotional activity that would improve the viability of your programme or service. What we will do is attempt to make that communication more informed if you are engaging in it for the first or second time. To do this we will be offering a short note on the core areas that we think need to be considered in the development of advertising and under what circumstances we ought to use it.

Consumer advertising

Advertising is the controlled voice of the institution, telling the public what it wants it to know and how it wants them to hear it. In this it has both an informative and persuasive purpose, which is the furtherance of the marketing objective. Advertising thus helps to position the institution and to develop a relationship with its audience. Its impact, of course, varies with the level of involvement of the audience and how carefully the message harmonizes with their needs, desires, fears and hopes.

Involvement is an interesting aspect of educational advertising. Basically the theory goes that high involvement by the purchaser in the purchase has advertising working in one way whilst low involvement leads to a different use of advertising and achieves its objective in different ways.

Given that the notion of education can entail both high and low involvement, the use of advertising and its frequency can be considered. For example the effects of advertising accumulate over time and reach a threshold that can be as low as three exposures before the message actually gets home. That is why advertising needs to be run much more than three times if it is to capture the whole of its target markets, and that is why direct marketing can be more effective. Regular exposure is important for advertising as it incubates habits that require further advertising to maintain them. This is a real problem on a smallish budget and where the public relationship can be so very important in the promotion mix. It can keep the name and values of the institution at a high enough level in public awareness to maximize the value of the short sharp burst of advertising that colleges and universities can afford around their prime recruitment date. But remember, particularly if contemporary images are being used, advertising is subject to obsolescence, which means it can need expensive renewal.

KEY DISCUSSION AREAS FOR ADVERTISING

How much to spend

Setting the budget depends on the objectives. Some media are much more expensive than others and some appeal more to certain groups. It is clear that the full-time student will listen more to the radio for instance than the middle-aged manager working in an office environment. To be sure you get the best result, understand what media your target market uses and then recommend them to the marketing team. Most institutions can fund small-scale advertising campaigns out of cashflow provided the returns in terms of fees are fairly immediate. For longer term brand building, resources may need to be built. Then the exercise becomes one of investment. Also consider sharing costs with other organizations whose own image would benefit from association with you. As with most aspects of the expenditure on marketing, it is difficult to quantify the return on the money spent. Arriving at the appropriate budget may have more to do with the negotiation within the budget process than in the content of the proposal.

Figure 7.1 classifies colleagues into four groups. Identifying which of your decision-makers fall into which box can help you to plan your strategy to secure the budget needed. Your line manager might well be a high supporter who is highly involved in the budget process, but try and make the heads of the institution's marketing departments aware as they will be the ultimate decision makers. It is always worth trying to convert financial directors into high supporters, for their opinions on budget, as we all know, often have authority beyond knowledge.

	Highly involved	Limited involvement
High support	Influential allies	Non-involved allies
Low support	Influential opposition	Non-involved opposition

Figure 7.1 *Identify influencers of the marketing budget*

Decide on the message and agree the creative treatment

Be sure of what you want to say, the tone with which you want to say it, and how the media works with the ideas generated. These ideas can be rational, emotive or moral but they must be grounded in what the institution is, not what you might want it to be. It needs to be desirable, exclusive and believable. Veracity is the best policy in advertising as in all other communications.

Just about everyone knows what a good advert is, regardless of experience, whether they are in the target market or understand the objective of the communication. Far better to leave it to the experts and give then a clear brief of what you want. That does not mean that you should stay quiet if the creative execution is clearly wrong – you ought to know the market, but be guided. Check who owns the power in this debate. Only the side that has the research which shows what the target market thinks can really win it.

Visuals that capture audiences

The following are some ideas to consider when developing print advertisements:

- Choose colours that connect your organization's identity. The simplest example is the logo colours of your college or university. It does not make sense to develop your brand in advertising and not use the colours that consumers may most readily connect with your school.

- Apply the billboard test to the piece as a whole. Could people read and recognize the information while driving? Some detailed information might be necessary, but are you capturing their attention to go further?

- Realize that people may forget lists of data, but they'll recall images. Just make sure that you don't let the graphics overcome everything else.

- Build interest. If you are creating a multiple page brochure keep in mind that the first couple of pages (even the envelope!) may determine whether or not the reader will lose or gain interest.

- Make the material progressive. Once again, if the piece is multifaceted, try to make the transition to the various areas in a consistent and smooth way.

Media selection and frequencies

We mention this above. The media and the message must complement each other. Indeed a range of communication themes on the key message might be developed to best suit the media being used. Media are expensive and professional advice is essential. Know what you want from the campaign and then find the media best able to deliver.

Table 7.1 is based on a chart published in 1995 by Kotler and Fox but with the inclusion of the Internet.

Geographical weightings

The nature of the offering will influence the choice of media. Local press and radio are ideal for informing the local community and obviously national or even international press can help if the audience is more widely dispersed. We have in mind here an evening class and a full-time MBA programme for instance.

Methods of evaluation

The methods relate to the objectives. If the purpose is to recruit students then, have you done so? If the objective is to generate enquiries about in-

Table 7.1 *Profile of major media categories*

Medium	Advantages	Limitation
Newspapers	Flexibility, timelines, good for local and national markets, broad acceptance and high believability.	Short life and poorest production.
Magazines	High geographic, demographic and occupational selectivity, credibility and prestige, long life and good pass-along readership.	Long lead time, some wasted circulation often no guarantee of position.
Internet	Specific, interactive and psycho-demographically specific and engages visual and audio senses.	Reach and expertise.
Radio	Mass use with high geographic and demographic selectivity, relative low cost.	Audio presentation only. Lower attention than visual media, transient and greater difficulty to respond.
Cinema	High geographic and demographic selectivity, focused atmosphere, attentive audience.	Expensive if not using existing visual ad, up against best exponents of the media.
Outdoors	Flexible, high repeat exposure, low cost and competition.	No audience selectivity.
Direct marketing	High audience selectivity, flexible, can personalise	Fairly high costs per item; issue of junk mail.
Television	Combine sight, sound and motion, appealing to senses, high attention, high reach	High cost, high clutter and fleeting exposure but multi-channel allows greater audience selectivity.

house programmes for employers, has it done that? These can be counted and classified as to their potential and ultimately as to their successful completion.

A range of tracking methodologies is available that relates to spontaneous and prompted awareness of the brand and the values that underpin it.

ADVERTISING FOR STUDENTS: A UK EXPERIENCE

The scramble for university places by students and for students by Universities and Colleges begins during the middle of August. The students who are at the centre of this are mostly those whose grades at 'A' level were not what was required to fulfil their conditionally offered university places. So we have a real market where students want to get as close as possible to their ideal course and institution and the institutions themselves need, financially, to fill their places whilst retaining their image and position.

The following analysis is based on three UK national newspapers appearing the weekend following the announcement of the results: on the Saturday, the *Independent* (containing the official UCAS listings) and the two others on the Sunday: the *Sunday Times* and the *Independent on Sunday*. Interestingly the Sunday Times had fewer institutional adverts for degree places and more for re-sit services than did the *Independent* newspapers.

All advertising institutions offered a mix of contact points, which included e-mail, open days (involving family if needed) and telephone. None appealed directly to specific segments in the market such as ethnic groupings. Some, like Nottingham Trent University, offered many messages within a common design and those like Lincoln and Humberside used the same strapline over different images of students. The messages were of six types:

- The basic informational advertising place where the stature of the institution is assumed. Typical were De Montford, Sheffield Hallam, Liverpool and Swansea.

- Those that challenge the student to apply but accept only those whose results would be compatible with the standing of the institution. Reading, Goldsmiths and Royal Holloway, Hertfordshire and Aberystwyth are typical. They positioned their offering on the basis of the institutions' outstanding record for innovation or heritage.

- Those that emphasize the customer service nature of the university or college, offering to support the aspirations of the student. These are mainly the newer universities and the higher education institutes such as Coventry and Cheltenham and Gloucester.

- Those offering new, innovative awards. Predominant in this group was Nottingham Trent which lead with its new university foundation degree a two-year degree from Greenwich, and new programmes from Sheffield and Sussex.

- Those who lead not on education but on social life and a comfortable atmosphere – Bradford and West Hertfordshire College.

- The immediate link with employment prospects, for example Kingston.

- The blatant hard sell and call to action of Greenwich and Somerset Colleges.

Here are examples of advertising messages for some of these groups (and we are making no implied comment on the quality and effectiveness of the advertisements by including them in this list – many, including those listed, are involving, interesting and inviting).

The puns

- 'APU a better choice of course' (Anglia Polytechnic University.)

- 'A greater degree of stimulation.' (London Guildhall.)

- 'Your course to the future.' (University of Wales, Newport.)

Self-interest

- 'Put yourself first.' (Sheffield Hallam University.)

- 'Call now and talk to an expert about your future.' (Liverpool University.)

- 'After all, it's your choice.' (Cheltenham and Gloucester College of Higher Education.)

Call to action

- 'Don't dream, achieve.' (Nottingham Trent University.)

- 'Right place right now.' (Somerset College of Arts and Technology.)

- 'Time…to change your life.' (Liverpool John Moores University.)

Problem solving

- 'Your future plans in a tangle?…let us help.' (Bradford College.)

- 'Relax, we have everything you need.' (Teesside University.)

- 'Phone a friend.' (University of Northumbria at Newcastle.)

Aspirational

- 'More than a dream.' (Trinity College Carmarthen)

- 'At Nottingham Trent we're constructing careers.' (Nottingham Trent University)

- 'What would you do with £50 million?' (University of Luton)

Advertising is a strong tool in building the brand but what is central to its success is what stands behind it. These concerns are well expressed by Sir John Daniel, former Vice-Chancellor of the Open University, who argued that unifying individuals through questions, rather than indoctrinating students with ready answers, is the real task of universities, and that dedication to that task, rather than a fixation on the short-term needs of employment, is also more likely to attract donors. For a more extensive review we recommend that you read *No Logo* by Naomi Klein (2000).

DIRECT MARKETING

Direct marketing is simply getting to customers on a one-to one basis to help them choose your offering. It involves response advertising and can use all the media ranging from the Internet to the letter. The choice is yours but success does depend on your audience being able to receive your message. Adverts in *The Times* might not reach *Sun* readers and Web adverts, regardless how well they are routed, do not reach non-Web users. In the next two sections we deal with direct mail and exhibitions, mainly because these can be undertaken without the whole institution being involved (although the marketing department might insist on exhibition involvement). The principles upon which success in these activities depend often transfer to other media given a sensitive appreciation of the relationship of the media with their users.

Designing and writing copy for the components of a direct mail package takes practice. If you're having trouble producing strong copy, you should seriously consider using an expert, if you can afford it. It is true there is no point in spending money on creating a strong product if the communication then fails it. To test the quality, ask the target group. At the very least get someone unconnected and uninterested in the programme or service you are offering and see if they can understand what you are offering. For direct marketing most people tend to write on too high a level and are too wordy.

It is easy to waste money on direct mail but, correctly planned and

83

executed, it can be one of the most cost-effective marketing vehicles at your disposal. American Express or the *Reader's Digest* spend millions and make millions. Their packs and continuous contact programmes are right for them. They are unlikely to be correct for you. This is not to say that carefully crafted packages including the institutions' main prospectus should not be sent, or that you should not keep in touch with those who register on programmes, nor are we saying that these activities ought to be less than professionally managed with clear objectives. What we are saying is that simple letters and pamphlets can have the desired outcomes if, and it is a big 'if', they are well produced and targeted at customers who are interested in what you have to say.

Indeed our experience has lead us to believe that the expectations of education customers can be fulfilled by well-written letters on the institution letterhead direct and personalized to the customers' needs. In the UK at least, the power of the signature from a perceived senior academic still carries an involvement level much higher than a similar approach from the bank manager!

Checklist for preparing a mailing shot

In preparation for the design and production of a mailing project make sure you know why what you have to say is important. You do need to believe in the offering as well as the customer who receives the mailing. And don't rush the reader. Remember, if what you have to say needs to be 'experienced', then encouraging visits might be the best outcome of the mailing – mailings don't achieve everything for you.

So how do you go about writing a direct mail piece? Does the mailing create the right impression? If it looks like junk mail this is the impression it will create when it is received. Does it have 'eye appeal' in that the recipient will want to open it? Is every letter fully personalized?

Is the copy written is such a way that the narrative is interesting and involving? Does it deal with the readers' desires or problems – and then offer solutions? To this extent creditable testimonials of people with whom the reader can identify – either as peers or as role models – can prove very helpful and persuasive.

In writing the mailing how may times have you used the word 'you'? Most successful packages use it many times for it ensures that you talk to your readers and not at them. The best way to maintain interest is to keep the sentences short and punchy. Keep the paragraphs to about ten lines and use the active voice rather than the passive. Try a warm involving style and use repetition to make sure the reader is aware of the benefits that responding to the mailing can bring.

It does not really matter how long the letter is providing you keep the reader's attention. You do this by being relevant to the needs of the reader. An employment contract can run to five or six pages and it always seem to keep our attention.

Make sure that the letter makes it clear what is offered to enrich the well-being of the reader or solve the problem. Present it clearly. If the programme involves long hours of self-instruction or regular attendance at the campus, explain it positively and in an up-front way. Raised expectations unfulfilled make an angry customer, not just a disappointed one.

Target your mailing well. This might be difficult if you are starting from scratch. Analyse existing users of the programme, who pays for them, where do they come from, what are the characteristics which make the programme appeal to them, and then look for more of the same. An alternative to general mailing lists is to target your mailing piece in journals, magazines or news-papers. Using journals can be a very effective form of international targeted marketing and, for a very focused market, can be very rewarding.

Make it easy to respond. Pre-paid envelopes, fax-back forms, e-mail addresses and telephone numbers all make it easier for the reader to respond when they first decide to and do it quickly. But then ensure you are able to accept the response format. If there is a telephone number make sure someone is there to answer it.

Pay special attention to the image. If you cannot afford quality then usually it is best not to proceed, although photocopied sheets in a plastic folder bearing the institution's logo can work well. The reasons are to do with it being compatible with prudent management and the gifting of something to the reader. Most people respect the obligation this gift creates when they accept it and will respond. This gift item also keeps the institution's name with the reader much longer than the letter itself.

If you are going to use a brochure here are a few tips:

- Use pictures and/or drawings to illustrate it and make the images dynamic.
- Give the institution's heritage and its philosophy so the reader has a feel for the institution with which they are dealing.

- Use real people undertaking the programme or using the skills and knowledge they have acquired. And be realistic. A friend of ours in the US, commenting on the number of racially mixed photos that are in institutional brochures and prospectuses in the US, said that 'sometimes black kids just want to hang out with other black kids'. Keep the images credible.

Zoe Whitby, director and consultancy services manager at Heist, one of the UK's best educational marketing organizations, gives the following tips based on her work for creating course leaflets:

- *Give the right depth of information.* Potential students want to know about the content of the course and they want it to be written in a language that they can understand. Include the hours of study, nature of the work involved, field trips, work experience/placements and social life. For part-time students, times of study and the cost are the priority.

- *Communicate your strengths.* Turn course features (for example, the course includes a placement) into benefits (our students complete a work placement – over half are offered jobs by their host company). Applicants are increasingly becoming focused on outcomes.

- *Colour, design and photography.* Good leaflets are not necessarily those that have colour photographs and expensive design (although many do fall into this category). It is better to be up to date with well-written word-processed information than to provide an outdated 'glossy' leaflet. If photographs are included, make them worthwhile by focusing on a simple strong subject; capture the moment.

- *Making the text accessible.* Be warm and welcoming. Show enthusiasm for your course and write in conversation style.

- Have a clear focus to each page with a heading across the top.

- Divide the text with subheadings that themselves convey messages.

- Use white space to avoid cramping text.

- Highlight strength in bold large text.

- Summarize key facts in boxes or bullet point lists.

- Use clear diagrams to explain structures.

EXHIBITIONS

Exhibitions are proving popular for the providers of services to the education sector and for institutions themselves. The notion is not new with those institutions engaging in international marketing, who are well aware of the advantages of well-positioned and well-stocked professional stands at international recruitment fairs. With domestic markets now requiring the same attention, institutions need to be well versed in the opportunities that exhibitions offer. They should plan to attend those that are most appropriate and, when attending, they should do so with a style that fits their image. Although the opportunities are great in being able to meet potential customers face to face, getting it wrong could mean that it is your last chance.

The exhibition medium:

● brings your most active potential students or customers to you (but they become better informed at the exhibition so they might also be the most demanding);

● allows you to demonstrate your service and products as well as creating some of the atmosphere of dealing with you;

● overcomes objections by addressing them directly;

● builds the brand as well as securing immediate commitments.

Stand design

Choices here depend on the budget (if it is not big enough do not go), your aims and your institution's image. Our advice is to visit exhibitions of all sorts, decide what you think is right for you and then meet with professional designers. The key is to be compatible with your own image. For small exhibitions the test is whether you and your colleagues feel embarrassed when standing in front of it. If you do, then do something about it! Clear good graphics are as essential as interesting content. Where possible, the content should be tailored to the site of the stand.

When exhibiting at large shows we recommend you consider the following:

● Ensure that your objective is the institution's offering not the design of the stand.

● Try to be distinctive.

- Avoid barriers that stop visitors walking onto your stand.

- Position your interesting displays near the edge.

- Assess whether the visitor understands your message in the three seconds it takes to walk past you.

- Good lighting can make a considerable difference.

- Use plants and foliage to soften the overall image – but not too much.

- When briefing designers, give them as much information as you can to enable them to achieve your objectives.

We strongly recommend professional participation in large-scale exhibitions, even given the skills of your graphics department. But if you are confident in the staff of your graphics department, and so are they, then use them. This gives the institution's exhibition team ownership of the stand, aids communication, and can bring the team together.

When you have made the commitment to the exhibition your purpose and aims need to be converted into clear objectives. There are a few simple principles that can be used to multiply the value of every exhibition and these follow. They are based on advice offered by the Association of Exhibition Organizers.

What to do before the show

Think it through and plan which exhibition is best suited for your needs, what you want out of it, how you will go about achieving that and how will you know that you have been successful. Certainly, setting specific goals helps, whether they involve the number of names taken, appointments arranged, or even the amount of signed up participation on the promoted programmes. Planning of the logistics is also important. Where will the stand be in relation to the flow of traffic? What will the design and the activities on the stand say about you and what you want to achieve? Also make sure your team is fully briefed on what is expected of them. Be explicit and cover dress, approach and attitude.

Make sure that those you have communicated with – the companies, schools and other institutions you want to see – know that you are at this exhibition. Recent research shows that 83 per cent of the most successful exhibitors at a range of exhibitions were the ones that took the trouble to mail their potential customers about their services before the show. This also means taking advantage of any pre-show publicity and advertising – make sure your know what media are reviewing the show and contact them directly. In your pre-show planning don't forget to consider the Web and see whether the show site can provide links to yours.

At the exhibition

At the show spend the optimum amount of time with visitors. We know this sounds a little harsh, but your institution has a plan and is paying both for the site and for your time so here are some further tips developed by the Association of Exhibition Organizers:

- Attract – stop people in their tracks. Use colour, motion, sound and bold graphics in stating the benefits you have to offer.

- Reject – politely filter out the wrong people for your purpose. Ask a few qualifying questions. 'Are you interested in our courses?' If the answer is 'no' then wish them a good day because you don't want to waste their day!

- Explain – get straight to the benefits of joining or working with you.

- Close – if you want an appointment make sure you get one. If you want a name and address, likewise. Get the maximum commitment and follow up.

Just a word of warning: as the *Scotsman* newspaper commented on 15 March 2000: the crunch question remains unanswered: 'with so much emphasis on marketing, will the "product" itself suffer?'

After the exhibition

To reap the rewards of the exhibition ensure that the team is debriefed and do it honestly. Elicit suggestions for improvements at future events. Remember to measure the specific goals you set out with and analyse (and publish to the team) the result, good or bad. Make sure you track the leads fast, because the chances are that others also have them to contact and being last creates the wrong image of how important they were to you.

The budget

Only you can judge what it is worth to attend a large or small exhibition. It can be a very expensive exercise. What is really important is that you do not exceed your budget by suddenly thinking of an idea, which you want to include in your stand, but was not thought through beforehand. To help with this planning and pricing we include a simple chart, which can act as a check-list and a budget-control document. Many items might not be appropriate but their inclusion gives you a chance to consider them before rejecting them. Table 7.2 comes from a useful book on exhibition design and management by Bittleston and Ralton (1995).

BEST PRACTICE IN THE US AND THE UK

Judgement as to the quality and effectiveness of advertising is, as we have previously mentioned, determined by whether the objectives were met and how the promotional activity enhanced the overall marketing of the institution. In the US, the Council for Advancement and Support of Education (CASE) also runs awards and has even more sections. We recommend that you visit the site at www.case.org.

In the UK, Heist run a competition annually to help spread good practice. We also recommend their magazine *Education Marketing*. There is also a further education network that exists to provide support and benefits for all marketing personnel in the post-16 education sector. Formed in 1986, the Marketing Network exists to support staff in the further education sector who have responsibility for marketing and student recruitment. It is interested in spreading best practice and offers a forum for it to be discussed.

Table 7.2 *Exhibition checklist and budget*

Item	Budget	Actual	+/−
Stand space			
Service to the stand			
Electrical installation			
Lighting			
Water and waste			
Insurance			
Stand design			
Design			
Building			
Transport			
Dismantling			
Storage			
Carpeting and ceiling			
Additions to basic shell scheme			
Furniture hire			
Floral hire			
Stand graphics			
Graphic design			
Print and product			
Application to stand			
Transport and storage			

Table 7.2 *(continued)*

Item	Budget	Actual	+/−
Communication and advertising			
Literature design and print			
Give-aways			
Press packs			
Catalogue advertising			
General advertising			
Poster and in-hall adverts			
Hospitality costs			
Telephone			
Staff			
Training			
Travel and parking			
Accommodation			
Stand staff food			
Badges			
Contingency			
TOTAL			

8

Public relations

According to the UK's Institute of Public Relations: 'Public Relations practice is the planned and sustained effort to establish and maintain goodwill and mutual understanding between an organization and its public.'

To encourage people to entrust their education and employability to an institution requires all those who are part of the institution to take responsibility for what the institution wants to be, is perceived to be and what in all veracity it is. That needs full commitment to a common goal. The first part of the chapter considers the issues of goodwill and reputation and then we turn to how public relations activities can help shape them.

GOODWILL

The political aims and accountability of a higher education system necessarily contribute to its reputation and the 'collective goodwill' held by its host and student communities. 'Collective goodwill' is used here in the sense of publicly held positive views of the reputation of the profession. It implies confidence in undertaking transactions with the profession.

Goodwill, unlike reputation, is taken to belong to the users of higher education institutions. Society's collective goodwill is the narrative of previous actions built from personal experience or accepted traditions and is used to reduce the uncertainty of the future. It is fragile and can be easily disrupted by deliberate ambiguity about the trustworthiness of the system.

REPUTATION

Reputation can be considered as the repertoire of expected behaviours held by the institution. It conveys information of economic value and it is in the interests of those who have good reputations to maintain them (Dasgupta, 1988). Reputation helps to categorize and maintain social order where personal trust through contact is difficult to establish or where one is unable to trust oneself to make a reasoned decision. It embodies the cumulative experience of, and feelings towards, an institution by the host community and offers to reduce the complexity and ambiguity of any anticipated interaction between the institution and the community. It has distinct exchange-facilitating advantages and a positive reputation has real social, moral and economic capital. The most obvious example of this is the importance of brands in the purchasing behaviour of consumers. Brands reduce the anxiety of choices.

Reputation, however, can be outside the perception or control of the institution that has the reputation. Even the maintenance of a reputation that is consistent and trustworthy among all of higher education's stakeholders may be problematic because of the traditional ethos of academia's anarchism and autonomous structure before mass higher education's imposition of managerialism.

Misztal (1996: 124) suggests that in order to establish and maintain a favourable reputation strong constraints must be imposed upon individuals to set aside individual interest for the wellbeing of the collective. She offers three mechanisms for this: 'formal control, moral commitment and societal pressure'. Of course these mechanisms must be contextualized through the type of institution and the expectations that the institution's stakeholders have of its reputation. There is a danger that only one mechanism will dominate and that formal managerial control will be imposed through external accountability and competence-based models. This could have a negative effect on higher education diversity, demolishing the mutual moral trust between the academic community and its new range of stakeholders, including the corporate body of the institution itself.

The rate with which the reputation of an institution will adapt to the repositioning of higher education will differ between those stakeholders who have closest contact with it, the students, and those who might have least, non-graduate parents of young children. Any changes that the sector makes ought to consider these differing rates of adoption. It is clear that a vice-chancellor might be fully aware of the need for a new mass higher education bargain with the state but for the first-generation undergraduate the degree still retains its elitist qualities.

THE INDIVIDUAL AND THE CORPORATE WHOLE

A danger for the higher education sector, which fosters institutional autonomy, is that its members have an incentive to act imprudently while trading on the reputation of the sector. This may have short-term benefits for one institution but, in the long term, it could destroy the sector's reputation and encourage the withdrawal of society's under-pinning collective goodwill. An institution carrying the generic label 'UK university' is given a level of personal and social trust beyond that normally given to other educational institutions (if this were not the case, the polytechnics would have had no reason to change their names) and, in accepting the role of a university, the institution owes its trusting host community a duty of due diligence. An institution that is economically coerced by aspects of its funding to lower its standards might gain short-term advantages. The impact on the goodwill towards the institution and, subsequently, the whole sector, takes time to enter the public domain. During the period between the transgression and the specific lowering of the goodwill towards the sector, the institution enjoys the benefits of the reputation given to all credentials of a certain type.

The response from higher education cannot be to wonder whether to co-operate with the state's changes. Rather, it should consider how to do so. The dilemma in such co-operation is for the sector to retain its reputation for academic autonomy and excellence and to negotiate a stronger reputation with the state to secure future funding. Gambetta (1998: 229) would acknowledge that an unwilling co-operation between higher education and the state will lead to the loss of trust between the parties but goes further to assert that any knowledge of the coercion will reduce the trust that others have in this forced co-operation. This 'introduces an asymmetry which disposes of mutual trust and promotes instead power and resentment'. As Baier (1986: 241) observes, 'Trust is much easier to maintain than it is to get started and is never hard to destroy'.

FROM TRUST TO PRACTICE

The best place to start with public relations is to define your public and how you are going to address them. Table 8.1 shows a matrix of publics to be addressed and the ways in which they can be reached. The list of publics is not extensive and more appropriate matrices can be used to fit the particular needs of a given institution or department.

The skills involved in delivering the activities listed in Table 8.1 are many and various. The following points may guide you in evaluating your institution's competence to work in these areas unaided.

Exhibitions

- Get a good position where the public must pass.

- Train and motivate the stand team.

- Don't do it on the cheap, you will look bad against competitors and demoralize your own staff.

Sponsorship

- Ensure the synergy works for the prime market and other markets.

- Consider negative as well as positive impacts.

- Find a way to measure the impact whilst understanding the full costs in detail.

In-house journals

- Should be of a high quality.

- Should use professional graphics.

- Should have an editorial team led by a powerful professional editor.

Overseas public relations

- Make your presence appropriate for the market; don't transfer from your home-based activities.

- Speak in the market's language.

- Make contact easy.

Table 8.1 *The PR planning matrix*

Activity	Host country	Students	Existing and current staff	Potential partners	Opinion markets	Competition	Donors	Facility
Exhibitions								
Sponsorship								
Journals – in-house								
Overseas PR								
Media relations								
Product placement								

Media relations – through training

- Know the media and those who work in it.

- Recognize the media's needs as well as you can.

- Be honest.

Product placement (mentions on TV, radio, and films)

- Dialogue with programme makers.

- Visit sets and studios.

- Prepare opportunity synopses.

Table 8.2 outlines some advice for writing copy.

Table 8.2   *If you are writing copy, here are some 'dos' and 'don'ts'*

Key 'Dos'	Key 'Don'ts'
Check spellings. Check spellings of names rigorously. Check titles, job titles, functions etc, nothing but the right words will do. When using lists, use uneven numbers. Hunt and kill the cliché. Put your subject into the context of now/today/this week. With verbs, use the active not the passive mode. When breaking a quote with 'he says', make sure the part before the break is strong enough to stand alone. Keep the subject and the verb together – as few words in between as possible.	Don't put ponderous job titles into the introduction. Don't start a sentence with a present participle. Don't start a sentence with a number eg '2,343 students …'. Don't muddle 'it's' with 'its'. Don't use quotation marks around words or phrases. Don't use italics, dashes, exclamation marks if you can help it. Don't use foreign words without good reason. Don't use 'etc'. Don't use ('…'), especially not at the end of a paragraph or piece.

For a really good start guide to using plain English read Martin Cutt's *Plain English Guide*, part of the Oxford University Press Quick Reference series.

There are four simple rules that we think apply to all the activities:

- Understand your target audience and talk to it. It wants be engaged in conversation. *But* don't do this in such a way that you alienate any other important audiences.

- Prepare fully and ensure that the activities are in line with the values of the institution. Expensively produced literature, when you are promoting to a poorly funded sector, can be counter-productive.

- Use experts. If you cannot afford them find another way of reaching the audience with the skills you have, or invest in training.

- Above all keep control. Have a common goal and make sure everyone and everything has that at its core.

Once you have audited your skills, decide how you are going to reach your audience. These decisions need to be co-ordinated through the PR plan.

There are four key aspects of any PR plan:

- Appreciate the situation. Know the facts; understand the institution's current reputation. If you do not know how your publics judge you and what that judgement is, then research them and find out. Research in this context both informs you of the current situation and can give you ideas and platforms on which to build PR campaigns.

- Define the objectives of the campaign. Is it to change the image of the institution or to influence the motivation you want to create in your students? Is it to influence potential staff or research investors? Is it to establish a notion of local community or to repair damage done to the reputation of the institution by staff or students?

- Define the publics and their relationship to your stakeholders – do you wish to influence the whole of the host community or just the owners and managers of the local public houses?

- Select the media through which you will attempt to achieve the change: Internet, press, radio, television, road shows or exhibitions. It is unlikely that any one of these in isolation can carry the message really effectively but each has a distinct role in an integrated campaign. For example, the printed press is usually the best media for hard facts and arguments; television is better for emotion.

Evaluation can be qualitative (for example, people speak more highly of the institution) or quantitative (there is more general interest in recruitment advertisements). Qualitative measures cannot necessarily be connected to a particular event that is responsible for a change in attitude and behaviour. More quantitative methods can be employed such as measurement of new enquiries at exhibitions, measurement of coverage in the media, and the use of opinion or attitude polls.

WRITING PRESS RELEASES

The press release is the most commonly used way of dealing with the press, both local and national. The design and issue of press releases involves much more than sending an important (to you) note to a media owner and demanding that it needs a wider audience. Many others have the same view of the importance of their communication. The chosen media know that and usually know their readership's interests better than you. After all, it is their job to sell the communications that the media carry to their market. The first consideration in offering your message is how it can help the journalist, and messages need to be framed with this in mind. They need not be of global importance. Press releases about first-class honours students to their local press with pictures of the student, university or even the university crest can be really effective, and so can the mature student who has achieved vocational success. Human interest is usually the key.

It is really important that, in the writing of the press release, you need to be sympathetic to the media's needs and empathetic to their audiences. You also need to get through the clutter of other people trying to do the same thing.

Here is a checklist of seven useful points to bear in mind when formulating press releases:

- Subject – make it clear early on what the story is about.
- Organization – who is it from and why is this of interest?
- Advantages of the content to the reader.
- Applications, if any, for the reader or for what the reader might be interested in (for example, national championships).
- Details of who sent it and how they can be contacted.

- Contextual information, or background information. This helps to trigger links for journalists or helps them to understand the importance of your message.

- Make the presentation of the release clear and distinctive, and type it double-spaced with a clear headline.

In order to be really effective the institution should ensure that all staff that are likely to engage with the media should to be professionally trained. Centralization allows the use of one well-developed distribution channel ensuring that all appropriate contacts in the press: local, national, international and trade are listed correctly by their areas of interest and influence for the college. These contacts also need to be kept up to date with the institution even where there is no story. Journalists need to be treated with respect, so visit them, invite them to functions and show them that you understand their needs and values. Time spent building a rapport is basic professional practice but can have real benefit when you need to explain issues or put your point of view. One such situation might be at a time of crisis, for example when students are hurt, or a lecturer is found with a bogus qualification, a poor quality assurance report is produced or almost anything that can become a crisis.

CRISIS MANAGEMENT

In today's more violent and litigious society, parents, educators and administrators are becoming increasingly responsible for managing crisis situations that occur in schools and colleges. The dramatic use of aggressive 'acting out' behaviour in the US is a complex issue and is undoubtedly related to changing patterns and values in society. Regardless of the causes, institutions are coming to accept that managing crisis situations is important to the reputation of the institution and, in extreme cases, to the safety of its staff. The cost of mismanagement can be very high. Post September 11, 2001 this has become increasingly important.

Prevention

Crises are of two major types: those that are non-life threatening and those that are. Both risks can be planned for by developing internal response plans. Steps that can be taken include setting up a crisis response team, carrying out an environmental and systems audit to test the rigour of the institution's social, and political standards to ensure appropriate policies are in place and that they can be rigorously defended.

In addition, the institution needs to know in advance what actions it will take and who precisely will carry them out.

De-escalation

Good media skills, and effective communications and information flows help to stop the crisis growing bigger than it needs to. In media responses be honest and should the crisis involve potential danger caused by others, try to quickly stabilize the situation before physical intervention is necessary. So alert all appropriate agencies, set up a crisis centre, help the media be honest and put the lives of any person above the reputation or physical structures of the institution.

Crisis intervention

If you need to negotiate to retrieve your management suite or release hostages then know what you're doing. It is important that the institution accepts professional advice and always conducts itself with dignity, valuing human rights and freedoms.

Post-crisis interventions

Hopefully this means coffee for the media and a little cleaning up. If events are more serious, ensure that counselling is provided if needed and is available quite some time beyond the incident. A major crisis will change the nature of the stakeholder relationships, so ensure that you are on top of it. Talk the crisis through and take the appropriate action to reduce the risk of it happening again.

The most important thing to do is to have a crisis management plan in place, with all the personnel likely to be involved trained and ready to act. Trial or 'dummy runs' should be held from time to time to ensure that the team works effectively.

Crisis management is often about mobilizing resources quickly and appropriately to resolve issues. In-house training is important to simulate these solutions and so is the use of public relations professionals. There is even an Institute for Crisis Management in Higher Education dedicated to sharing information on crisis response, located at the University of Florida.

9

Student recruitment

Kotler and Fox (1995: 393) state that: 'Students provide most educational institutions with their reason for being.'

Enrolment management encompasses both the recruitment of new students and the retention of continuing students. Often institutions have not used available data to understand who stays and who leaves or to develop retention strategies. In this chapter we will deal with the application of marketing principles and we will include examples and references to sources of help but, before you contact them, you need to formulate the questions that you need to have answered. You need to plan what kind of students you want, what the attributes that enhance the institution are, why you need the students, what you can offer them and how you are going to keep them.

The notion of diversity of college and university missions is very important to the richness of the sector but this is only true if the institutions live their mission. An open access institution that is found to have lower than average enrolments from a particular ethnic or socio-economic sector, or from mature or part-time students, is clearly not living up to its mission. The same may be said of an institution that favours research achievement over teaching. Distinctiveness in corporate mission is attractive to students but faking or deceit is not. The image of the institution needs to be clear to students so that they may have some idea of what they are buying with their time and money. So, the first point in the recruitment of students (and of research students and staff) is to plan what you want to become and then carry out the plan. For many that might mean throwing out the complex but beautifully bound corporate strategy and starting from the reality of an existing position grounded in the market for students they have taken.

Question why students are attending your institution, what you provide for them and how you could do it better. You can always change the position, course by course, department by department, but know first what you are now.

When we know what we are, we can begin to build a proposal to attract students. Many techniques have been tried from vice-chancellors photographed in public houses astride bucking broncos to cinema advertisements and local television slots. All of these can make a valuable contribution to the image of the institution and this message can be effectively delivered to your market via direct mailshots, school visits, department open days, and Web site development. The media can all be valuable provided we know what impact they have in contributing, directly or indirectly, to the attractiveness of the benefits we offer the potential student. They need to be targeted and evaluated.

ATTRACTING THE STUDENT

The design of an integrated market plan goes beyond a well-designed and delivered promotion plan. It goes into the realms of the institution as a product in itself. What are the core perceived attributes that help students decide to attend the institutions? They might include the scenic location or the city or campus location, but what these attributes are and how they influence decision makers needs to be unpacked.

Locality might be important for part-time students if they are even to be able to attend. Closeness to work or home is often important to them. Locality might also be important because it is close to a national centre not of learning but of nightlife! It might even be important, in the UK, that the local soccer team is doing well! Some of these factors are out of the control of the institution but others, such as expense and the style of accommodation offered to students, are within the control of the institution. Indeed the best attributes that the institution may have to offer is not its rated research team but its accommodation, bar and sports teams.

So if location is a crucial deciding factor for your potential student cohort then ensure that you understand what they desire and how they want to engage with it. Once you understand then, if possible, exceed their expectations. For the more mature student, the quality of your taught programmes might be the critical factor. The global move to performance indicators will make the institution's performance in these areas ever more transparent and so resources need to be put behind those features that the institution is best able to influence. These then need to be marketed to those you feel have best competitive advantage. Securing student first choice status really does help planning and ensures that the whole institution uses its resource to its best advantage.

Also make sure you know who makes up the market. It might not just be the student who registers at the beginning of term. The student or staff member may often seek advice from others so it is important to understand whose endorsement they are seeking as well as the decision framework. If these attributes cannot be accommodated then dissonance occurs that delays decisions and causes concern after the decision is made. Post-purchase dissonance is likely to happen on any major purchase that involves considerable commitment.

THEORIES OF THE CONSUMER

The question of 'who is the consumer of higher education' is complex. The education experience is undertaken by the student, who is usually considered the consumer, but it may not be the student who selects the experience or the institution, and it may not be the student who pays for it. If society's needs are considered, the student may be only one of the actual beneficiaries of the education product. Parents and family represent other possible consumers, particularly as purchasers. They often constrain the choice of institution and substantially underwrite its costs. The family is not generally a significant beneficiary of the student's education, except by sharing in whatever symbolic value it may provide. Society at large substantially underwrites much of the cost of the education experience and might be considered the consumer. Its interest is more generalized, but more utilitarian in that it wants an educated citizenry and an educated workforce of a certain magnitude and level of preparation.

It is important to observe and allow for alternative channels of communication and incentives to elicit responses from the market. Those with fewest monetary resources also have needs for consumption, some of which can be met in non-market exchanges through social networks. In other situations they may resort to using political channels rather than market interaction to communicate needs, resulting in various forms of government interaction in the market. Regulation may be used to modify some consumer barriers, for instance, or public agencies may be created to provide products in a way and at a price that the market does not, as in the case of public education at all levels. Such interventions assume a posture that is sometimes adversarial to the market and its participants.

In higher and further education, as with some other complex industries, communication through the market can be slow and highly ambiguous. In the market for student enrolments, the consumer and the product are not clearly identifiable. If the consumer is specified as the individual student, and if students were able to freely select the specific education experiences they desired, programmes would look different. Parents and society, as consumers, usually articulate much broader preferences. They want meaningful degrees, an assortment of skills, and distinguished achievement.

The market for students is highly segmented, suggesting that consumers are communicating their preferences. There are segments for a great many individual programmes and degrees, and for a wide range of institution sizes and types. American higher education, for instance, is considered the most diverse in the world. This array of choices has occurred through entrepreneurial entry and identification of niche demand, and through consumer choices expressed through the market. Where consumers have lacked access to desired programmes because of cost or other barriers, they have moved politically to have those programmes implemented at some public cost, or have passed laws requiring removal of particular barriers, such as prejudicial admissions and disability barriers.

Society is concerned about the number and qualifications of graduates, but the interaction with the community is more complex. Institutions and those who use them both assume roles of producer and consumer, and often the community is unaware of the nature of this relationship with an institution, or is unaware that it may be participating in a market exchange. The institution must work harder to determine the value aspects of its offering in the exchange, because the community is less adept at revealing them. The shaping of an offering on the part of the producer requires an understanding of consumer needs. This calls upon the producer to consider the implications of the offering for the experience of the consumer.

THE CONSUMING EXPERIENCE

One approach to the consumer is to examine the experience of consuming, rather than simply the decision to purchase (Holbrook, 1987). The idea of separating the purchase decision from the act of consuming has less relevance, perhaps, for retail oriented marketers, but it is significant for service marketing and instructive in considering the consumer in higher education. Consumers are primarily engaged in consuming behaviour rather than buying behaviour, and consuming is not a decision or brand choice activity. The behaviour of consuming focuses on intangible factors rather than tangible ones, and represents investment of time, effort, and ability, as opposed to money. There are also complex emotional components in the experience of consuming. Finally, whereas decision behaviour regarding product choice is conveniently bounded in time, consuming behaviour may not be.

The decision experience for the traditional student, including campus visits and other preparatory activities, may extend over the space of a year, but the consuming experience is substantially longer and more intensive. The investment involved for the consumer is monetary, to be sure, but higher education is consummately experiential. The consuming experience may be attached to objects and activities, which are tangible and directly observable phenomena, but the objective of the experience is quite intangible and barely measurable in many of its important dimensions. The real consuming activity is the engagement of some cognitive and affective change. The durability factor also suggests that the consuming behaviour – the use of the education experience – does not end with conferral of an award. It extends to some degree throughout one's entire life.

The consuming experience for grant and contract funders is more structurally bound, but the experience for donors does extend beyond the decision to bestow. Donors receive recognition and certain benefits, many of them intangible, from their beneficence. Successful appeals to donors are known to give particular attention to donor experiences.

INFORMED CONSUMERS?

We have avoided much standard textbook marketing in this book but, having introduced consumer behaviour, we want to consider two critical elements: informed consumers and the degree of involvement in the decision made. Informed consumers, because of their knowledge, are assumed to make rational decisions about their consumption behaviour, seeking to satisfy their needs and desires. However, those who pass for informed consumers in many sectors clearly make decisions with incomplete information. Educational institutions have made major strides in providing information for students, enabling donors and other stakeholders to realize the consequences of their choice and this is good. The brash advertising for chocolate bars is acceptable for this product group for in most cases the consequences of a wrong decision are minimal. Consumer education, is different and great restraint is required.

A high degree of involvement in the decision assists good decision making. If something is important to you, you are more likely to put more resources (particularly time) into making the right decision. For the student this is not as obvious as it might seem, given that the student's future is at stake. It might seem that following in father's or mother's footsteps is 'the only real option open' – or better than the other alternatives. Or a student might choose a short course for social rather than scholastic reasons. High-involvement deci-sion-makers are often the ones most institutions want to attract for they have consciously investigated their options and made their informed decision, and in doing so are more likely to stick with the course or institution they have chosen. High-involvement decisions are usually those that reflect upon the self-image of the decision maker (hence the change of name from 'polytech-nics' to 'universities' in the UK in 1992). They can involve personal or economic sacrifices and often carry a risk of getting it wrong. All these attrib-utes are present in the less long-term decisions about which logo to wear on a pair of shorts or which team to support or which books to say you have read. Education is not outside the power of the brand/self-esteem interaction.

So how do students make the decision about an appropriate institution for themselves? Table 9.1 gives some clues.

Table 9.1 *On what information source students decide on their Colleges and Universities, USA and UK*

USA (1998)		UK (1999)	
Internet	3%	Current students	75%
Current students	16%	Guides	65%
Alumni	7%	Internet	31%
Campus visit	24%	League tables	40%
Publications/mail	21%	Parents	89%
Parents	15%	Teachers	85%
Reference book	10%	Uni. prospectus	97%
Teachers	15%	Visits	90%

THE EFFECT OF EXPERIENCE

Another influence on the decision-making process will be experience. Those with experience of making a particular or similar decision will make quicker choices than those with no experience. But don't underestimate the speed of choice. Often, the quicker the decisions are made, the smaller the number of attributes that contribute to the choice. This has little to do with the amount of information available or even how accessible it is. The content of the selected and restricted number of options that are usually used to make decisions is what is important. Indeed, if we did not reduce our complicated and complex world into small chunks, knowing we are forgoing opportunities, we would be hard-pressed to take any action at all. Being in this 'choice set' for the target student groups is really important. If you are not in it, you are not even considered. This is one of the real problems that the Oxford and Cambridge colleges suffer from when they attempt to widen participation. Once you are in the choice set, it then becomes important to know who else is in it in order to position your proposal to its best advantage. It is even more important to recognize that you will not always be chosen but that you must remain within the set for your desired students. This argues for targeted marketing, shaping your communication to the attributes of the students you want. This sophisticated marketing is missing from much university and college literature, which seems to treat the whole of the potential student market as a homogeneous mass.

TARGET MARKETING

Selection criteria vary considerably between individuals and organizations, those who are buying courses for themselves and those buying for their employees' benefit. Taking the individual student first, getting into a particular choice set requires understanding of both the direct and the indirect influences on the decision-makers. As Figure 9.1 shows, some of the different contributors to the purchase decision can be:

- the initiator who suggests a reason for learning and for taking a programme;
- the influencer – the one who carries the authority of special advisor in the reference group the student consults;

- the decider – usually the one who pays, either in terms of time or some other resource (in organizational purchases this might be the human resource manager rather than the student);

- the user, who takes the programme.

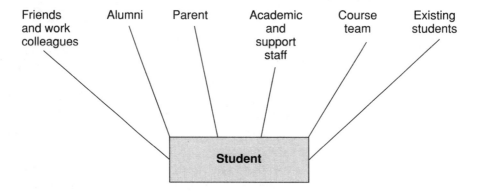

Figure 9.1

In Figure 9.1 many people might play one or any of the roles in the decision-making process and so the institution ought to have strategies to influence the impact of each of the groups.

Influencing these groups first requires understanding about what their perceptions of you are on the criteria upon which they make their choices when asked for advice. This is not an easy task. You must then change the reality and perception of the key attributes upon which the selecting group make their judgements. This might involve absolute or relative changes linked to others in the choice set. It might even mean trying to move the decision timetable. In the UK, universities offer unconditional offers only to students who have obtained the final entry requirements to an institution. Offers are usually made before the quantifying qualification is obtained and are conditional on them. Some colleges might decide to make unconditional offers on the findings of other assessment criteria from earlier qualifications such as the UK AS levels. This might change the image held of the institution by the student, for it could be interpreted as showing that the institution really wants the student. This might be appealing because it would reduce the pressure on achieving specific grades in final examinations and so might make the student more disposed to the institution. It might very well enable some institutions to be more successful at recruiting appropriately qualified student than is currently the case.

We have tended so far to concentrate on students purchasing programmes of study to achieve large substantial awards such as degrees at undergraduate and postgraduate level. Colleges and universities offer much more to their adult markets. The development of work-based learning, continuing professional development and just-in-time training and advisory programmes is becoming ever more important. The way in which the consumer buys, however, is likely to involve the same issues as discussed above.

The marketing process does differ where the transaction is not with individual learners but with other organizations. Organizations buy goods and services to make a profit, so the interest in a programme that you might be proposing to run ought to have a benefit that secures or increases their profit, or helps them to realize their societal and legal obligations. Here the decision-making is longer and is usually more complex. More people are involved in the actual decisions – this is particularly true as the size and cost of the training, consultancy or educational contract increases. It will often require more energy and time to secure success and it means adopting the commercial template of behaviour that is familiar to the purchaser. The critical success factor will include professionalism, flexibility, location and speed of delivery. The reputation of the institution will be important but secondary to the outcomes required of the training or consultant project. In business-to-business transactions, ensure that the value gained by the consumer is explicit and measurable, talk business and behave within your mission.

10

Fund-raising

RELATIONSHIP MARKETING: THE BASIS OF TRUSTING RELATIONSHIPS

It is generally accepted in marketing that it costs more to attract a new customer than to keep an existing one. This has placed new emphasis on the nature of the relationship between producer and consumer. The result is the concept of relationship marketing, which allows the producer to engender repeated exchanges with the same consumer by establishing a relationship of trust and communication, and to understand how better to shape the offering to suit consumer needs.

The goal of relationship marketing is to maintain consumer satisfaction over time. This can be defined as consumer-perceived value, which is the ratio between benefit and sacrifice as perceived by the consumer (Ravald and Gronroos, 1996). Total costs to the consumer may include indirect costs for such concerns as delayed delivery and distance to service, and psychological costs, which can include purchasing effort and aggravation, unsatisfactory interactions with the producer, and worry over producer commitment or behaviour. Once again, market research may be used to collect data about what is important to the student and ex-student, perhaps using the satisfaction inventory process in Table 10.1.

Further and higher education fits the profile of producers who can benefit from the relationship marketing approach (Tomer, 1998). It has the ability to make long-term commitments to students, donors, grant-funders, and communities. It seeks harmonious, non-opportunistic relationships, and it is a

Table 10.1 *Measure satisfaction more precisely with the Student Satisfaction Inventory*

Noel-Levitz, www.noellevitz.com

Student satisfaction inventory

Designed for annual use, the student satisfaction inventory asks students to rate the importance they assign to 70 statements about your campus, such as 'My academic advisor is approachable', 'Nearly all of the faculty are knowledgeable in their field', 'Tutoring services are readily available'. Unique to this instrument, students also rate each of the 70 items a second time to indicate how satisfied they are with the service specified.

A blueprint for action

The results of this precise two-step approach are remarkably revealing. In rank order, you learn which items should be at the top of your retention agenda; items that are of high importance, yet are not currently satisfying, to your students. You also learn which items need less attention. In effect, you get a blueprint to improve retention.

---

high service provider rather than being primarily dependent upon transactions.

A relationship marketing approach focuses upon close study and interaction with the consumer over time in order to tailor the value in offerings to suit consumer need. Institutions that use such an approach to students, for example, should exhibit reduced exit transfers, greater completion rates, and increased long-term student commitment. A relationship marketing approach to those communities or social groups from which students are primarily drawn would seek to hone the education product offerings to meet their needs as a constituency. A relationship marketing approach to the community should serve to enhance the local environment in which the institution operates by helping it to become more responsive to community needs. It is clearly advantageous to maintain strong relationships that lead to repeated exchanges with donors and grant and contract funders. As a consumer, the institution is subject to relationships with suppliers, and welcomes relationships that allow it to shape the offerings more to its particular needs. The latter relationships are typically more highly structured, particularly in state institutions, but this does not preclude ongoing relationships with suppliers that are mutually beneficial.

The potential for students/consumers to select alternative institutions/producers has increased in recent years because of programme standardization and variation in the pool of target students. In effect, each term's enrolment represents a return purchase by, or exchange with, the student. Students might, in the future, easily transport course credits from one institution to another to fulfil common requirements. It is true that degree programmes do exact some penalties for moving around, and the closer to the degree award, the more difficult the move, but student mobility has, nevertheless increased.

In terms of relationship marketing, institutions concerned about the retention issue would acquire deep knowledge regarding consumer needs through investment in an interactive relationship with the target students/consumers and their sociocultural context. They would then examine the total offering of the education experience for its composition of consumer-perceived value. Benefit elements would be as enhanced as possible, and the sacrifices demanded of the consumer would be minimized. Students often encounter unanticipated or indirect costs, and experience many psychological costs above and beyond the academic coursework. They frequently run foul of bureaucratic systems and unhelpful staff, for instance. A relationship marketing approach to students regarding tuition and fee increases in recent years might have mitigated the image of higher education as greedy and insensitive. The approach would have tried to find ways of adding value that would improve the net consumer-perceived value to the student and family. It would have also attempted to find ways to communicate the constraints upon the institutions more effectively.

THE IMPLICATIONS OF SPONSORED ASSISTANCE

Most institutions these days, even if described as state colleges or universities, are better conceptualized as state-assisted rather than state supported. This worldwide phenomenon is changing the nature of the relevance of state-sponsored education and the change has been typified in universities by the raising of tuition fees. This shift brings into focus the need for a professional fund-raising staff dedicated to the future of the institution to sustain its contribution to its community, both locally and globally.

Fund-raising has reached different stages in different countries. In the UK there is still a stigma associated with begging, whereas in the US fund-raising has risen to the status of development. Of course, the development of any relationship during its early stages is built on transactions. These transactions seek to establish a basis for trust and mutual understanding and do so by the exchange of tangible and intangible benefits. The relationship flourishes when the benefits exchanged are considered to be of real value. Fund raising is no different and, to be successful, a fund-raising culture needs to be developed that believes in what it can offer to donors and goes about securing mutual advantage in a professional manner. This requires a systematic approach, a plan that reaches into the future and that has the commitment of the whole institution, not only of the chief executive. (Although this can be very important as the achievements of a retiring President of Harvard showed by his part in raising £1.7 billion during his nine-year presidency.) It has to become a way of being for the institution and a way that the institution is happy with and able to handle. It is the opposite of the knee-jerk reaction to a deficit, which spurns the idea of fund-raising on a more regular basis.

Flynn (1980) has developed a model to contrast the development orientation of fund-raising with that of the narrow project-determined fund-raising orientation and his work is adapted in Table 10.2.

Table 10.2 *Contrast fund and development orientation*

Development	Fund-raising
Basic approach ● integrating ● focus on top quality education ● public relations are pre-requisite ● goals and objectives written daily ● stakeholders and public involved	*Basic approach* ● panic, crisis are factors ● limited, short-term objectives ● negotiation from a position of weakness ● fragmentation
Programmes and projects ● many and various – endowment, capital ● practice and policy manual ● stewardship programme	*Programmes and projects* ● many and various but small ● magazine sales, sports events ● lack of public debate ● monies absorbed into the institutional funds
Results ● large donation received on consistent basis ● work from a clear 5-year plan ● annual report to all stakeholders	*Results* ● failure to get everyone involved ● high staff turnover ● raising money on a crisis basis

FUND-RAISING ACTIVITIES

Selling, not exploitation, is a professional activity and one we ought to do well. So if we can't sell what our institution has to offer then perhaps we are in the wrong institution or we have failed to change what inhibits us from selling the institution. In either case we ought to do something about it.

Not surprisingly the leaders, both in hard cash and culturally, are the Americans and much of what we have to say can be enhanced by conference attendance, Web site interrogation and reading the growing number of texts produced. So like any other process of matching needs with outcomes, institutions must understand who their target markets are, how to organize to successfully penetrate them, how and what image to present to gain their involvement and, having put in all that effort, how to evaluate the outcomes of resource allocation. By what we have said we imply that fund-raising is everyone's responsibility. We believe that, but we also believe that specialist fund-raisers can make important contributions to the success of an institution's goals. Certainly more British institutions are coming to that view.

In starting to build a plan for our fund-raising activities it is helpful to consider why people donate money to education. There may be many and various reasons but we suggest that the five of the most common are:

- gratitude to the institution;
- affection for the institution;
- a desire for personal 'immortality';
- a sense of obligation;
- a tax break.

Each has its own relevance to the individual and by understanding each, and how the institution can fulfil the motivation, the institution can begin to target people and corporations who might benefit from donating to the institution. In building a list of potential donors, closeness to the institutional aims and values is a good indicator of affinity with the institution. This affinity can stretch from being a successful ex-student, to mutual use of an intellectual resource. Once the canvass list is developed, the approach to potential donors has to be planned. The following points are useful in preparing a fund-raising approach:

- people give money to people;
- people give to educational opportunities;
- people tend to give money to success;
- people give because they want to;
- people need to be asked.

The team for fund-raising includes all the staff. Chancellors, principals and their senior staff are all required to aid the effort. Networks are encouraged and used. And it takes hard work, not only to get the Vice Chancellor out or the Principal to give a speech to local business but also, once an ethos is generated (and the skills developed), to sell a consistent message based on the image of the institution – and this is where our previous thoughts on reputation become even more important.

When we say that fund-raising is an institution-wide activity we do not mean that all donor monies should be equally allocated regardless of the effort put in. There will be donor preferences and there will be specific activities undertaken by faculties that deserve to retain the major share of the funds secured. As with any other income-generation activity there are corporate overheads – not least in retaining and building the reputation of the institution – and they need to be paid for.

Most of this will sound familiar as an American model of fund-raising, and it is. In a country where the corporate rate of giving to higher education is 20 times that of the UK, this has to be the place where we look for good practice. We could argue that the culture and the internal financial structures are different in the US but this has been recognized and the UK government has made a start on making philanthropy tax-efficient, but a culture shift is not just the government's responsibility. Indeed the great voice given to industry in developing learning programmes might be the catalyst to ignite greater contact with commercial and educational institutions, leading to higher levels of financial support.

Having decided to approach fund-raising as an institutional culture issue, how should the institution organize itself? When starting this business (for that is what it is) you need to establish the closest network of potential donors and work outwards. It is important to track recent alumni too, but they are unlikely to donate when they are still paying off their student loans; alumni are a long-term business. Records on past students may not be arranged to facilitate this canvass but they can be prepared to be effective tools and will repay the effort put into their preparation. At the other extreme, the Chancellor or Chairman of Governors could be persuaded to donate and, if approached enthusiastically, might provide their own very fruitful networks. In fact, it might be worth starting the project with the senior officer – and the fund-raising office could not do better than report directly to the most influential (whether external or internal) member of the governing body.

What are the form and content of the proposals put before potential donors once they have been identified? Earlier we stated that donors can be motivated by a wide range of incentives. You need to convert these incentives into satisfying and distinct products from your institution, school, department or faculty. In so doing, some will appeal to large donors and others to small. The big, wealthy ego might need a library or wing of a science building whereas ex-students might just like to contribute to endowments for other students.

CORPORATE DONATIONS

Having designed your products to match your needs and the motivations of your donors in a way that is appealing, then the selling process begins. If a large donation from an individual or corporation is required, then the selling process is modelled on corporate selling. This starts by identifying customers, interesting them in the proposition, writing proposals (amending them to fit the financial situation of the donor) waiting for responses, usually compromising, and then, hopefully, receiving the big cheque.

The process can be – and often is – more complex. To save embarrassment the fund-raiser clearly should check that the institution is happy to accept the outcome prior to approaching a donor or corporation. It helps if your corporate marketing is focused and well directed. It costs more to prepare a personalized proposal, so some selectivity is required. This can be gained by applying the matrix in Figure 10.1 to the corporate contacts that might show an interest in supporting the institution.

Clearly, corporations that fit into the top left-hand box are your prime targets. If in placing local, national and global potential donors you find the bottom right-hand corner most populated, your problem is that they just don't know what you can offer and you are probably not skilled enough yet to tell them in the language to which they can relate. In such circumstances,

		Giving potential		
		High	Medium	Low
Interest potential	High			
	Medium			
	Low			

Figure 10.1 *Satisfaction inventory*

begin a campaign to raise the status of the institution so that they realize there are benefits from being interested in it.

SMALLER DONATIONS

At the other extreme to the large multi-million donations is the mass marketing to active alumni who may be prepared to provide small sums for student endowments. The gifts might be small but these people can be really important as supporters and advocates for the institution. One of the best ways of building alumni loyalty is through magazines, either paper or virtual. The real problem here is commitment and expense. Once you embark on this route it is difficult to turn back and the competition is huge. Why should we have a greater affinity with our school, college or university? Who contributed most to our current success? Not only that, but everyone from our bank and supermarket to our specialist interest groups wants us to identify with them. It is not that we are against building alumni databases and using them – quite the reverse – but do it with your eyes open. The Web site is probably now the best medium through which to recruit and maintain contact. It is interactive and can be more cheaply made and updated than the quarterly magazine. It can also automatically give you a response mechanism to maintain the accuracy of the list and an opportunity to research the changing interests of those on the list.

Do not underestimate the potential of your alumni's generosity. In the US there is a perceptible trend where the most significant amount seems to be coming from individuals with allegiances to a university and not from corporations, which tend to spread their donations across a range of institutions.

PLANNING THE CAMPAIGN

Table 10.3 gives a framework to help build an integrated fund-raising plan. Each heading ensures that goals are set and outcomes are measured. The first column helps us to identify appropriate markets and the approaches that might best be used to secure their support. Not all campaigns achieve an immediate financial return – indeed they may not be designed to do so. It is helpful, however, to record all benefits that can be attributed to the campaigns. The final three columns are a simple evaluation mechanism. It is worth keeping them updated so as to learn systematically from all the experiences of fund-raising in which you engage.

Table 10.3 *Funds raising framework*

Objective performance				Campaigns		
Constituent	Goal	Actual	Non-marketing benefit	Strength	Weakness	Action
Major gift						
Board						
Parents						
Alumni						
Business						
Faculty/staff						
Others						

Source: 'Evaluating the Annual Fund' Catholic School Management letter

11

E-education

BEHAVIOURAL CHANGE

> In the coming decade marketing will be re-engineered from A to Z... the successor to the Industrial Society – the Information Economy – will penetrate and change almost every aspect of daily life. The digital revolution has fundamentally altered our concepts of space, time and mass.

This is how Philip Kotler (1999) begins the final chapter of his book *Kotler on Marketing*. He goes on to consider how consumer buying behaviour will change and how business buying and selling behaviour will change, and he suggests ways in which companies might use the Internet.

Every day in the media there is a new story suggesting that classrooms and lecture halls are as good as finished. The Association of Teachers and Lecturers commissioned research from Alan Pritchard at Warwick University, published in the summer of 2000, which suggested that virtual teachers and computers that guide children through lessons could transform the face of classrooms within 20 years. Schools will become 'learning spaces' where face-to-face contact between teachers and pupils is strictly limited. Mr Pritchard does point out, however, that teachers will still be needed to ensure that students are protected from and guided through the vast amount of information available on the Web. And computers and technology learning aids will not replace the vital role of schools in helping children to develop social skills. Indeed there is some evidence perhaps that these skills are already on the wane if we listen to the complaints from employers that new employees are ill-equipped to deal with communication and team working. However, we cannot help but be excited by the prospect of integrated learning systems that lead students through computer-based lessons at their own pace with interactive capabilities and correction and marking along the way. Indeed, with the broadening of curriculum and government-inspired drives to bring more people back into education and to encourage lifelong learning, allied to teacher shortages particularly in scientific subjects and specialist areas, it may be that the ability to share between institutions through electronic means will be essential.

WHO CAN BENEFIT?

There are more than 100 million people worldwide with access to the Internet and traffic is apparently doubling every three months. These Internet users are not only young people. Large numbers of people are rapidly getting used to accessing information, learning where to look and following up links. They are increasingly starting to do business on the Internet. For those who are office based with a PC on their desk (or home based or travelling around) flexible learning is available to them now. A survey by Hewlett Packard Education revealed that 60 per cent of people (with access) have used the Internet as a medium to undertake training at least once. Much of the training is IT related, but management and interpersonal skills courses can be accessed and studied. The Internet allows 'just-in-time' training, letting you study what you want, or what your employer requires, when you want. You do not have to go to a classroom or leave your desk and you can take your education in bite-sized chunks.

Meanwhile educational broadcasting is increasing and improving by leaps and bounds. Greg Dyke in his *Spectator* lecture when he became Director-General of the BBC made it very clear that the BBC has ambitious plans to build on its historic reputation for educational broadcasting. Huge resources are being devoted to it. Educational broadcasting is going digital and interactive. It meets the government agenda of driving forward the technological capacity of schools. Major competition in the shape of Granada, Pearson and even Anglia TV is also moving fast. They all emphasize that what they are doing is making teachers' jobs easier by providing sophisticated support tools and learning aids and saving them time.

Jack Welch, oft-quoted Chairman of GE of America reputedly said, 'When the rate of change inside the company is exceeded by the rate of change outside the company, the end is near.' Is there a danger that the excessive rate of change in the world at large will alter things so much, and bring new and powerful players into the market, so that it threatens the future existence of universities and colleges? We do not think so, but it does significantly affect the way in which institutions both manage and market themselves if they are to retain their pivotal importance in the provision of education and training. Let us not forget that the Internet originated as a tool for academics to exchange ideas, so there is nothing new in it for them. But they need to harness it to enhance their offering.

The Web has really only been with us since 1994. Since then the explosion of dot.com companies rushing to take commercial advantage of an exciting new medium is starting to wane. People have made and lost a lot of money. It is time to consider what the real value of e-commerce is, where it will grow and prosper, and where it will simply support existing resources.

THE IMPACT OF CHANGE ON INSTITUTIONS

It may be important to get a good deal of the internal infrastructure for the anticipated changes operating efficiently and to ensure that institutions are capable of handling the increase in response speed required by the new medium. There may be significant costs involved.

Perhaps the most important thing to consider is that, in some ways, the need to respond to change may be driven from the home. In America up to 85 per cent of young people (who are connected) access the Internet only from home, not from school or college. The shortage of hardware, phone links, dedicated lines, and a lack of teacher training mean that this is not going to change quickly.

However, the search for information about education and training, courses, fees, registrations and admissions will increasingly be sought electronically and institutions need to be prepared to respond appropriately. The following checklist may serve as an outline of the areas that will need attention:

- improving internal processes and infrastructure;
- communicating within a college environment;
- communicating between departments and staff;
- use of ICT to enhance or deliver courses;
- Internet and extranet links with partners and communities;

- links with suppliers;

- uses for distance learning;

- staff development and training;

- ownership, development and maintenance of the Web site;

- the short and medium term investment decisions;

- ability to develop and grow organically, and the need for appropriate partnerships.

Michael Stoner of Lipman Hearne (a marketing and communication firm in America) points out that people are using online 'research' to inform their choice and purchase decisions. The actual purchase may be made in conventional ways but the key difference is that people obtain advertising and information 'on demand' – the customer can choose to receive information. Access from home will be important to education institutions because the audiences they are trying to reach will be online – potential students and their parents, adults seeking continuing education, and even alumni to keep in touch. We will steadily see the development of a variety of services that can be personalized to suit the individual – intelligent agents and the so-called 'push technologies'. The news agencies are an example of this: a consumer can specify a topic of interest, and a search engine can seek out appropriate articles using keywords and then forward them to an e-mail address. This can be paid for commercially and advertising can be attached.

THE CONSUMER RULES

One area in all this that we will all need to be sensitive about is that where consumers are choosing to access information, they may be less amenable to having linked advertising foisted upon them as well.

There are a whole series of implications in this for those responsible for the marketing of institutions and the courses they run. A rapidly increasing number of consumers are familiar with and use the commercial Internet, so the idea of a Web site and its uses already influences their behavioural patterns, particularly when they are searching for information. This is particularly true of young people. So it will be important to observe what happens in this commercial arena in order to understand what seems to work and what does not in an educational environment. The new Internet age offers both opportunities and threats. The main opportunity is that if we understand and accept the propensity of the Web it could revolutionize the traditional way in which schools and colleges interact with their students. The threat is that if we do not embrace the opportunity we may die. In addition the growing emphasis on 'lifelong learning' will drive the unitization of educational material to the point where much of it can only be effectively administered electronically.

Increasingly, the organizations most affected will be those that trade information rather than commodities. To gain real advantage, however, it will not be viable simply to use the Internet to process traditional courses, publications and interactive learning and 'marking'; we will have to change the business processes fundamentally so that they embody the technology from product inception through delivery and quality control. E-business requires a much tighter integration of process and technology between the institution (or business), its customers, suppliers and partners. It should be developed in such a way that it allows rapid alignment with customer choice. The implication of this is that existing business processes may need to be re-engineered to support and integrate with the chosen e-business model.

COMPETITION

Competition is already emerging. The world of education and training is a sector that will continue to grow. Mergers, acquisitions and strategic online alliances are taking place more frequently, and it is no coincidence that education content providers and media channels are coming together. Giants like Pearson coming together with NSC, Granada Group acquiring NFER-Nelson and Letts will quicken the pace. The UK government is determined that the University for Industry (UfI), or Learndirect as it is now branded, will take advantage of the accessibility to learning that the Internet brings, but that it will also try to do it on a commercial basis. So it wants to negotiate with colleges and other potential training providers to take a substantial proportion of the income available from delivering courses, support materials and qualifications – or it can and will go directly into the home and workplace.

Kotler (1999) gives four principles to be followed if we are to win in the new electronic age. These apply as much to educational institutions as they do to consumer or industrial product and service companies.

First, build and actively manage a customer database. The more you know about your students and potential students the better. All enquiries need to be logged, classified and made available for future use. We often talk about the 'cradle to grave opportunity' within education. Once students are in your system, the potential for directing appropriate new learning opportunities towards them as they move through life could be very valuable, and potentially increasingly acceptable to a population keen to progress in employment and develop transferable skills.

Second, develop a clear concept of how the company should take advantage of the Internet. Kotler lists seven ways of using the Internet:

- to do research;
- to provide information;
- to run discussion forums;
- to provide training;
- to conduct online buying and selling (e-commerce);
- to provide online auctioning or exchanging;
- to deliver online 'bits' to customers.

The organization's Web site must be appealing, relevant and current if it is to attract repeat visits. We all know of numerous sites that are none of these things, and we believe that investment in graphics, sound, and video (multimedia) will be necessary to ensure continued interest. Being up-to-date means at least weekly updates and references to 'coming soon', 'watch this space' and 'news' to stimulate repeat visits. Continuously and critically evaluate your Web site to ensure its relevance. Put your company banner on related Web sites.

Third, consider where else your potential students are likely to be searching or seeking information. Don't just put advertising banners on those sites, but consider offers that encourage potential customers to visit you, even if they are just modest promotions or free competitions – remember you are likely to be fighting to be noticed on a Web page.

Fourth, be easily accessible and quick in responding to customer calls. America On Line (AOL) received very bad word-of-mouth criticism back in 1997 when its subscribers could not get on line or reach the provider for help.

Just as many companies are getting their telephone customer response centres working really well by using modern technology, we are heading for a change in the speed and detail that enquirers might expect from e-mail messages. If you work in an e-mail office environment you know only too well that the moment an e-mail is transmitted to you, the sender not only assumes you have got it but have read it and are considering an instant response.

Kotler adds a useful chart that simply states how marketing will change into cybermarketing. This is reproduced in Table 11.1. The grid applies equally to products or services, and it is particularly appropriate for college marketing people and faculty staff because it points to the variety of services that can be personalized for individuals or small groups of individuals. The nature of college communication is such that there is a need to build medium- to long-term relationships with students or with alumni. Observing how businesses have been reacting and using the Internet is useful for developing college programmes. Because of the growing consumer reliance on the Internet, it means that a Web site too is already becoming a commonplace concept to them.

So we are operating in a world where there is a familiarity with the medium, but also growing frustration about the time it takes to find what we want, and disappointment with what we find – or cannot find. So quality, content, accuracy and being up to date are really important. But being able to be found easily is equally important. If you are not up to date on a course schedule for example, in the US and perhaps soon in the UK, you may find yourself facing a lawsuit.

Another good tip is to continue to design for low bandwidth users. Everybody talks about the excitement and benefits that will be available from 'broadband' but it will be a while before a significant number of people are capable of taking advantage of it. So minimize the amount of media and maximize the amount of information. Give the consumer the choice about whether to access audio or video files or 3-D technology.

MAKE ACCESS EASY

We have already talked about the importance of knowing who your audiences are, what they want and what they use the Web site for, and the messages that you are getting from their e-mails to you. Of course it is difficult to develop personalized services for students or potential students but it is possible to repackage material that is already in existence or that

Table 11.1 *Marketing output comparison*

Marketing activity	Traditional marketing	Cybermarketing
Advertising	Prepare print, video or voice copy and use standard media vehicles such as television, radio, newspapers and magazines. Usually only very limited information can be presented.	Design extensive information and put it on the company's Web page and buy banners and other sites.
Customer service	Provide service five days a week, eight hours a day in the store or over the phone in response to customers calls; provide on-site visits to maintain or repair.	Provide seven day, 24 hour, service response; send phone, fax or e-mail solutions; carry on on-line dialogue, repair problems from a distance through computer diagnostics.
Selling	Phoning or visiting prospects and customers and demonstrating product physically or by projective equipment.	Videoconferencing with prospect and demonstrating product on computer screen.
Marketing research	Use of individual interviews, focus groups and mailed or phoned surveys.	Use of news groups for conversation and interviewing e-mail questionnaires.

is being generated in the college and make it available to those who want to receive it. Make it easy for them to find it by using 'headlines' like 'education', 'business', 'careers', 'lifestyles', 'new courses', and 'health'. We constantly find that, despite considerable awareness of the Web in organizations, and despite them possessing their own Web sites, material in-house is still produced in the same old way and has to be 'converted' to make it suitable for Web transmission. Everything should now be written in such a way that transposition to the Web site is automatic. Do not underestimate how difficult this is in most organizations. You must remember that institutions are being judged against commercial Web sites. It has got to be good. Business is taking it seriously and professional marketing or corporate communication departments are responsible for the Web site – not the IT department or enthusiastic amateurs.

Institutions must view Internet communication as strategic communication and develop Web sites and other resources accordingly. The strategic issue is to establish what are the strengths of the college and you can communicate them through the Internet. Having done this you still need to make sure that whatever is developed is capable of being marketed in the other media.

One of the more interesting marketing opportunities for a college of further education or for a university is to try to cultivate relationships with children and their parents by developing high quality material now – before commercialization takes the prospect away through game-based fun products. You are generating potential students for the future.

You must maximize the transaction capabilities of your site. To be ready for e-business will require a deliberate and strategic effort throughout the organization. People will need to become as competent at using the Internet as a tool as they are with the telephone, fax or postal service. It is most important to consider partnerships or strategic alliances with other organizations that can facilitate orderly development and strengthen the overall offering. It is unlikely that you will be able to do it all on your own.

As an enterprise pursues a commitment to e-business, it must include all the IT and business process re-engineering implications or it will not meet performance expectations for fulfilment and service. In addition, the organization must avoid moving out ahead of the business by implementing a physical infrastructure ahead of the development of an appropriate business model. If it does there is a high risk that costly investments will have to be made that do not meet the needs of the e-business proposition and its cost structure or that could have been more efficiently obtained from an outside supplier or partner.

It is particularly important to decide how involvement with e-business will be managed within the institution because that will largely dictate the pace at which development will proceed, the level of commitment and the eventual success. Four common models are:

- *Committee.* This is a loose group of managers and 'experts' from around the organization who are used to considering and making recommendations. The existence of such a committee probably implies that the organization is really not ready to 'go for it' but feels a need to demonstrate its interest.

- *Centre of excellence.* A central team is formed dedicated to the task of delivering e-business. Its members may work with project teams in different parts of the organization to ensure consistency and best practice. They are often concerned more with uniformity, efficiency and cost than with groundbreaking development.

- *Company champion.* A single very senior individual has overall control of 'making it happen' throughout the organization (and the budget). This individual needs the authority and power base to succeed in this to avoid the inevitable departmental attitude of 'not invented here'. So it needs to be a mature and stable organization.

- *Separate entity.* Setting up a separate business unit may speed up development and lead to innovative new thinking, but this runs the risk of the main organization losing intellectual capital or even control.

Whichever route is chosen it is important that any Web-based development and the existing IT infrastructure are in harmony.

There are many books that can assist with the 'how to do it' aspects such as choosing the right software, creating Web pages, minimizing the time it takes to access your home page and move on from there. But perhaps the two most important aspects to remember are to put an infrastructure and organization in place that allows you to update your Web site daily, and to make use of the technical experts in this field to help you properly analyse your needs and specify the most appropriate systems. A simple evaluation chart can be used here and is given in Table 11.2. Do not just fill in the boxes; revisit it every few months to see whether you are improving as it is a useful health check.

Another checklist, adapted from customers.com, asks a variety of questions about your approach to the use of the Internet to assist and retain students:

- Are you targeting the right students?

- Do you have a profile of current and prospective students?

- Are there student segments you do not reach, and would online delivery help?

- Which segments will benefit most from online delivery?

- How accessible are these students? Do they have the technology and skills to participate?

Table 11.2 *Evaluation of infrastructure strengths*

Aspect	Rating (eg out of 10)	Comments
Download speed		
Ease of navigation		
Ease of search		
Interactivity		
Transactional		
Information content		
Branding		
Novelty		
Visual appeal/design		
Up to date		
Overall		

- Can existing programmes be converted to meet online needs or are new programmes required?
- Do you own the student's total experience?
- Do you map current interactions?
- Is the student experience with the institution seamless from initial enquiry to the conclusion of course or transaction?
- Are the administrative processes designed to make every student transaction easy and responsive?
- Have you streamlined business processes that impact on the student?
- Do you audit current functions?
- Which processes are designed from a student's perspective? Can all be conducted on line?

- Which processes can be improved to make them easier?
- Are processes shared with other parts of the institution, or outsourced? Do you evaluate level and quality of service?
- Can you provide an all-round view of a student relationship?
- Can both student and authorized staff have electronic access to the complete records of the student?
- Can information be quickly updated by all participants?
- Who owns the student database?
- Can students help themselves?
- Are there adequate navigational tools and propensity for interactivity?
- How many services (content, admissions, registrations, payment and so forth) can students complete online?
- If students hit a problem, can they get 24-hours-a-day help?
- Do the processes help students to do their job?
- Do both administrative and academic staff understand the student goals and rationales for selecting online courses or information?
- Can staff build one-to-one relationships to assist, help and advise?
- Can you deliver personalized services?
- Do you question students about further topics and areas of interest?
- Do students give feedback on current programmes – academic and administrative?
- Are alumni regularly contacted for periodic updates?
- Can you identify loyal student supporters and enthusiasts for your courses?
- Do you foster a sense of community?
- Can students 'chat' away from the administrator or faculty?
- Is this continued beyond a specific course?
- Does the institution's Web site offer other value-added information or processes to enhance the community of learners?

References

Baier, A (1986) Trust and Antitrust, *Ethics*

Barnett, R A (1994) *The Limits of Competence*, SRHE and the Open University Press

Barwuah, A and McCallum, I (1999) Community profiling to improve college responsiveness, *FEDA Report*, **2**, p 11

Belk, RW (1988) Possessions and the extended self, *Journal of Consumer Research*, **14**, pp 139–68

Bittleston, D and Ralton, K (1995) *Beating the Drum: How to exhibit effectively and get better results*, Forbes Publications

Black, S (1995) *The Practice of Public Relations*, Chartered Institute of Marketing and Butterworth Heinemann

Blake, N, Smeyers, P, Smith, R and Standish, P (1998) *Thinking Again: Education after postmodernism*, Bergin & Garvey, Westport, CT

British Council (1999) *Realising Our Potential*, British Council

Bruner II, G C (1988) The marketing mix: time for re–conceptualisation, *Journal of Marketing Education*, (summer), pp 72–77

Carpenter, P (2000) *eBrands – Building Internet Business at Breakneck Speed*, Harvard Business School Press, Boston, MA

Chong, Y Y and Brown, EM (2000) *Managing Project Risk – Business Risk Management for Project Leaders*, Financial Times, Pitman Publishing, London

CIHE (1998) *Partnership for the Professions*, CIHE

Coates, D (1998) Marketing of further and higher education: an equal opportunities perspective, *Journal of Further and Higher Education*, **22** (2), pp 135–42

Dasgupta, P (1988) Trust as a commodity, in *Trust: Making and breaking co-operative relationships*, ed D Gambetta, Basil Blackwell, Oxford

De Chernatory, L (1999) Brand management through narrowing the gap between brand identity and brand reputation, *Journal of Marketing Management*, **15**, pp 157–79

De Chernatory, L and Riley, FO (1997) Modelling the components of the brand, *European Journal of Marketing*, **32**, pp 1074–90

Doyle, P (1994) *Marketing Management and Strategy*, Prentice-Hall, Englewood Cliffs, NJ

FEFCE (1998) *Marketing: A good practice guide*, The Stationery Office, London

Field, J and Moseley, R (1998) *Promoting Vocational Lifelong Learning: A guide to good practice in the HE sector*, HEFCE

Flaherty, MG (1987) The neglected dimension of temporality in social psychology, *Studies in Symbolic Interaction*, **8**, pp 143–55, JAI Press

Gambetta, D (1988) Can we trust trust? In *Trust: Making and breaking co-operative relationships*, ed D Gambetta, pp 213–37, Basil Blackwell, Oxford

Gurviez, P (1997) Trust: a new approach to understanding the brand–consumer relationship, *AMA* (June), pp 505–18

HEFCE (2000) *Diversity in Higher Education: HEFCE policy statement*, HEFCE

Hess, JS (1995) Construction and assessment of a scale to measure consumer trust, *AMA conference*, pp 20–26

Holbrook, MB (1987) What is consumer research? *Journal of Consumer Research*, **14**, pp 128–32

Holcomb, JH (1993) *Educational Marketing*, University Press of America, Lanham, MD

James, C and Phillips, P (1995) The practice of educational marketing in schools, *Educational Management and Administration*, **23** (2), pp 75–88

Johnson, H (1996) Education Marketing: for Academics, for 'Anoraks', for Everybody? Conference paper, *Policy, Process and Practice*, pp 67–74

Klien, N (2000) *No Logo*, Flamingo

Kotler, P (1999) *Kotler on Marketing: How to create, win and dominate markets*, The Free Press

Kotler, P and Fox, K (1995) *Strategic Marketing for Educational Institutions*, Prentice-Hall, Englewood Cliffs, MJ

Kotler, P (1987) Humanistic marketing: beyond the marketing concept, in *Philosophical and Radical Thought in Marketing*, eds AF Firat, N Dholakia and RP Bagozzi, Lexington Books, Lexington, MA

Kumar, N (1996) The power of trust in manufacturer–retailer relationships, *Harvard Business Review*, (November–December), pp 92–106

Laczniak, GR and Murphy, PE (1993) *Ethical Marketing Decisions: The higher road*, Allyn & Bacon, Boston, MA

Maklan, S and Knox, S (1998) *Competing on Value: Bridging the gap between brand and customer value*, Financial Times/Pitman Publishing, London

Maylor, H (1999) *Project Management*, Financial Times/Pitman Publishing, London

McKenzie-Mohr, D and Smith, W (1999) *Fostering Sustainable Behavior*, New Society Publishers, Gabriole Island, BC

Mick, DG (1986) Consumer research and semiotics: Exploring the morphology of signs, symbols and significances, *Journal of Consumer Research*, **13**, pp 249–92

Misztal, BA (1996) *Trust in Modern Societies*, Polity Press, Cambridge

Nicholas, G (1997) *Collaborative Change in Education*, Kogan Page, London

Piercy, N (1992) *Market-led Strategic Change*, Butterworth Heinemann, Oxford

Roberts, D (1999) *Pricing Research Techniques: Adapting commercial practice for education*, HEIST Publications

Ryans, CC and Shanklin, WL (1986) *Strategic Planning, Marketing and Public Relations and Fund-raising in Higher Education*

Schmitt, B and Simonson, A (1997) *Marketing Aesthetics: The strategic management of brands, identity and image*, The Free Press

Sowrey, T (1987) *The Generation of Ideas for New Products*, Kogan Page, London

Symes C (1996) Selling futures: A new image for Australian universities, *Studies in Higher Education*, **21** (2), pp 133–47

Symes C (1998) Education for sale: a semiotic and analysis of school prospectuses and other forms of educational marketing, *Studies in Higher Education*, **42** (2), pp 133–52

Trow, M (1996) *Trust, Markets and Accountability in Higher Education: a Comparative Perspective*, seminar paper given at the SRHE, Oxford, June

Zanzig, BR (1997) Measuring the impact of competition in local government education markets on the cognitive achievements of students, *Economics of Education Review*, **16** (4), pp 431–41

WEB ADDRESSES

Marketing agencies

http://www.marketinged.com – Marketing Higher Education

http://www.ama.org – American Marketing Association

http://www.becreative.net – Bergeron Creative Company

http://www.educ.org – Australian Education Management

http://www.educationmarketing.org – Education Marketing

http://www.heistco.uk – Heist Consulting

http://www.higheredconsulting.com – Higher Education Consulting Directory

http://www.idp.edu – IDP Education Australia

http://www.marketinged.com – Topor Consulting Group International

http://www.noellevitz.com – Noel–Levitz, Marketing Consultancy

http://www.scannellkurz.com – Scannell & Kurz, Inc

http://www.stamats.com – Stamats Communications

Marketing information

http://www.dfeegov.uk – Department of Education and Employment

http://www.britcoun.org – British Council

http://www.bublac.uk – Journal of Marketing for Higher Education http://www.baolco.uk – British Association for Open Learning

http://www.case.org – Council for Advancement and Support of Education

http://www.cheba.com – Consortium for Higher Education Bench-marking analysis (CHEBA)

http://www.universitiesuk.uk – Representative body of UK heads of universities

http://www.fedaac.uk – Further Education Development Agency

http://www.forrester.com – Forrester Research

http://www.jupiter.com – Jupiter Communications

http://www.qaaac.uk – Quality Assurance Agency for Higher Education

Exhibitions

http://www.educational-netco.uk – EMAP

http://www.exhibitionsworkco.uk – Association of Exhibition Organisers

Software

http://www.blackbaund.com – Blackbaud Europe

Index